BIG QUESTIONS IN HISTORY

Harriet Swain is Deputy Features Editor of the
Times Higher Education Supplement and editor
of *Big Questions in Science*.

Big Questions in History

EDITED BY
Harriet Swain

VINTAGE BOOKS
London

Published by Vintage 2006

2 4 6 8 10 9 7 5 3 1

First published in Great Britain in 2005 by
Jonathan Cape

Vintage
Random House, 20 Vauxhall Bridge Road,
London SW1V 2SA

Random House Australia (Pty) Limited
20 Alfred Street, Milsons Point, Sydney,
New South Wales 2061, Australia

Random House New Zealand Limited
18 Poland Road, Glenfield, Auckland 10, New Zealand

Random House (Pty) Limited
Isle of Houghton, Corner of Boundary Road & Carse O'Gowrie,
Houghton, 2198, South Africa

The Random House Group Limited Reg. No. 954009
www.randomhouse.co.uk/vintage

A CIP catalogue record for this book
is available from the British Library

ISBN 9780099468462 (from Jan 2007)
ISBN 0099468468

Papers used by Random House are natural,
recyclable products made from wood grown in
sustainable forests. The manufacturing processes
conform to the environmental regulations of the
country of origin

Printed and bound in Great Britain by
Cox & Wyman Limited, Reading, Berkshire

Contents

Preface

Historians ask questions all the time but it is rare for them to tackle directly the really big ones – What wins wars? What makes a great leader? How do intellectual movements start? – particularly in just a few pages. Usually, they are restricted by the need to produce detailed evidence, to qualify their assertions, to note exceptions and other points of view, to keep well within the boundaries of their personal expertise. This book has invited them to cast their inhibitions aside and venture an opinion on some of the general historical themes that most people are likely to have pondered from time to time.

Some have looked for clues in many periods of the past, and across several continents, others in a particular time and place. In the process, boundaries between history and politics, philosophy, social science, theology and other disciplines have often dissolved. Each writer has nevertheless found some kind of answer.

But it is only one answer. So journalists have also been asked to provide a context, exploring how other historians and thinkers have tackled the same questions in the past, highlighting some of the most controversial aspects of each question, and looking at new areas of investigation. Their commentaries are a mere taste of the many different directions that historical enquiries have taken over the years, and of the key people involved.

Thanks to all the journalists and academic contributors for taking on such huge questions so gamely, to Mike North, Val Pearce and Sonia Allen, and to Mandy Garner, features editor, Gerard Kelly, deputy editor, and John O'Leary, editor, of the *Times Higher Education Supplement* for their support and time. Thanks too to Will Sulkin, Jörg Hensgen and Chloe Johnson-Hill at Random House.

Harriet Swain

What is history

What is history?

Richard J. Evans
*Professor of modern history
at the University of Cambridge*

? The answer to the question 'What is history?' seems obvious enough: history is the study of the past. But, of course, it is not quite as simple as that. There are some ways of studying the past that cannot be classified as history. History is, in the first place, the study of the past in order to find out the truth about it. Unlike novelists or film-makers, historians do not invent things that did not happen or conjure up characters that did not exist. Playwrights and screen-writers can change the raw materials they use when they are dealing, as often happens, with a topic drawn from the past to make the subject more interesting and more exciting. They can make up dialogue, insert words into historical documents that are not in the originals, and generally use their imagination in a manner unfettered by the constraints of the historical evidence. Historians have no such luxury. They deal with fact, not fiction.

This distinction has been made by all historians ever since the first serious historical work to come down to us from the ancient world, the *History of the Peloponnesian War*. Its author, Thucydides, rejected the romantic myths purveyed by the poets and checked all his evidence, as he told his readers, 'with as much thoroughness as possible'. But he went on to complain, as historians have done regularly ever since, that the truth was far from easy to discover: 'Different eyewitnesses give different accounts of the same events, speaking out of partiality for one side or the other or else from imperfect memories.'

In the two and a half millennia or so since Thucydides wrote his great work, historians have elaborated a whole battery of sophisticated methods of checking the evidence and dealing with the gaps and partialities of their sources. But they can never attain perfect or total knowledge of the whole truth. All they can do is establish probabilities – sometimes overwhelming, sometimes less so, sometimes hardly at all – about parts of the past: those parts that can be accessed by means of the remains it has handed down in one form or another to posterity.

History only ever involves a selection of what is knowable about the past because it has a second essential quality apart from the search for truth: it aims not just at reconstructing and representing the past but also at understanding and interpreting it. This is what makes history different from chronicle, which tells the tale of the years, marking off events as they happened, but does not try to make any connection between them or attempt to explain why they occurred.

The centrality of explanation and interpretation to history also makes its approach to the past different from those of religion, morality and the law. Religions seek legitimacy through sacred texts handed down by prophets or their disciples from the distant past. To treat such texts historically, however, means to put their sacrality to one side and to question them just as one would question any other historical source, a procedure undertaken most powerfully by the greatest of the historians of the Enlightenment, Edward Gibbon, in his *Decline and Fall of the Roman Empire*.

Moral and legal approaches to the past are concerned with judging guilt or innocence and assigning responsibility for actions that are classified as good or evil, lawful or criminal. These, too, are unhistorical ways of dealing with it. In recent times, it has become fashionable to categorise historical figures from a time such as the Third Reich, or the Atlantic slave trade, or the European settlement of Australia, in terms derived from morality and the law: as 'perpetrators', 'victims', 'bystanders', 'collaborators' and so on, and to distribute praise and blame accordingly. This is profoundly alien to the enterprise of history, which is concerned in the first place with explaining why people did what they did, with causes, effects and interconnections, not with issuing arrogant verdicts on complex moral issues based on the luxury of hindsight.

Of course, historians can, do and in many cases have an obligation to provide raw materials, evidence or background briefings to assist institutions such as war crimes tribunals or commissions assessing claims for compensation for legally recognised historic wrongs, just as another important side of their work lies in producing scholarly editions of previously unpublished documents. But such a deployment of expertise, however necessary, is not the historian's main business. The historian's job is to explain; it is for others to judge.

This means, among other things, that historians have to try to understand the past from as wide a variety of points of view as possible, not to see it through the eyes of one particular contemporary or group of contemporaries, still less to study it exclusively in the light of the concerns of the time in which they are writing. History written purely to fulfil a present-day purpose, such as encouraging national pride or showing that one ethnic or national group has been oppressed over the ages by another, is all too likely to degenerate into propaganda unless it is held in check by a willingness to bow to the dictates of the evidence where the evidence runs counter to the historian's purpose.

Nevertheless, at the same time, history also inevitably involves formulating hypotheses on the basis of present-day theories and testing them critically against a thorough review of the evidence. Historical perspectives on the past change, not just with growing distance in time but also with the changing ideas and interests of historians themselves and the developing ideas, methods and concerns of the intellectual world and the society within which historians live. That is one important reason why, over the years, history's scope has been steadily expanding. The days when it was concerned solely, or even principally, with kings and battles, politics and diplomacy, 'great men' and great wars are long gone. In the twenty-first century, everything is grist to the historian's mill.

Big questions involve the history of private as well as public life, of ideas and beliefs, of personal behaviour, even of broad topics such as the environment, geography and the natural world. They can be asked about any part of the world, any era of the past. All with one proviso: research into these areas is history only if it really is undertaken in search of the answer to a 'big question'. History is not, and never has been, the mere accumulation of facts and knowledge for their own sake: that is better categorised under the heading of antiquarianism.

Of course, historians have always disagreed among themselves about virtually all of these points, as they have about most answers that have been put forward at one time and another to big questions about the past. Controversy is an indispensable means of advancing historical knowledge, as the rough edges are rubbed off implausible or exaggerated interpretations, and reasoned debate consigns the unsupported argument to the dustbin of discredited hypotheses. The pervasiveness of controversy among historians is one reason why politicians are always wrong when they claim that 'history' will absolve them, judge them or vindicate what they have done. Historians will probably never agree about issues on which national leaders have made such claims, whether it is the Cuban revolution or the second Iraq War.

The historian's training can generate a healthy scepticism with which to puncture the wilder claims of politicians and statesmen. It can, or should, help anyone who undergoes it to spot a fake when they see one, and to demand clear evidence for a statement before they accept it. Training as a historian is essential for a whole variety of jobs in the heritage industry and more than helpful in the wider field of culture, tourism and the arts, which generate a far higher proportion of national income and export earnings than the manu-facturing industries do nowadays. History books, tele-vision shows, radio broadcasts, magazine articles and other cultural products have never been more popular. History in this broad sense is a major national eco-nomic earner.

But its most important justification lies in its less immediately tangible effects. History can teach us about other societies, other beliefs and other times, and so make us more tolerant of differences in our world. And it can provide us with a democratic civic education to help us to build a better world for the future.

Further reading

David Cannadine (ed.): *What is History Now?* (Palgrave Macmillan, 2001)

E.H. Carr: *What is History?* (1961), 40th anniver-sary edition, with an introduction by Richard J. Evans (Palgrave Macmillan, 2001)

G.R. Elton: *The Practice of History* (Sydney, 1967; 2nd edn, with an afterword by Richard J. Evans, Blackwell, 2001)

Richard J. Evans: *In Defence of History* (1997; 2nd edition with Reply to Critics, Granta, 2001); *Telling Lies about Hitler* (Verso, 2002).

Commentary by Harriet Swain
Deputy features editor of the Times Higher Education
Supplement

It was E.H. Carr who most famously asked the question by making it the title of his 1961 collection of essays, *What is History?*. But he was certainly not the first person to put it. Historians have been wondering about what they are doing since the fifth century BC, when Herodotus stated in the preface to his work that it was to preserve a memory of the deeds of the Greeks and the Barbarians 'and, in particular, beyond everything else, to give the cause of their fighting one another'.

While few of his successors have felt the need to spell it out, the idea that history is about commemorating important events – particularly those involving fighting – and explaining why they happened, has endured, though not alone. Since Herodotus, historians have suggested numerous other definitions of what history is, from what actually happened in the past, to television reconstructions of royal love lives.

The study of the study of history, however, is relatively recent, relatively rare and sometimes controversial. Shouldn't historians be getting on with explaining the past rather than agonising about why they are doing it? And if they spend more time analysing history than writing it, how can they speak authoritatively on what history is all about?

For many early historians it was much simpler. History was about man's relationship with God – no question. Sacred Hebrew texts continually looked to the past to identify the hand of God in particular events, and early Christian writings did the same. Probably best known for his 'sacred history' is the fourth-century writer and philosopher St Augustine, whose *City of God* painted a vision of history as the unfolding of God's will – a view that influenced Western historical writing for hundreds of years.

Religion also inspired early Islamic historians, driven by the desire to produce accurate and detailed accounts of the life of the Prophet, and here an important emphasis was establishing the authenticity of historical sources. This was one of the preoccupations of Ibn Khaldun, a fourteenth-century Islamic scholar, who had a great impact on the future study of history in the East and West.

Big Questions in History

His world history, *Muqaddimah*, was before its time in studying psychological, economic, environmental and social forces in history, and he was also an early advocate of comparing the past and present to help understand a society.

The political philosophy of Niccolò Machiavelli (1469–1527) is sometimes linked to that of Khaldun and interest in studying and authenticating ancient texts was an important part of historical study during the Renaissance in the West, but for Renaissance historians like Machiavelli it was the ancient classical world that explicitly shaped the way they thought about history. Machiavelli followed classical authors in the belief that history should provide moral guidance and should employ a persuasive rhetorical style in order to do it.

The idea of a moral purpose to history persisted through the European Enlightenment, in spite of God as a guiding force behind human affairs being discarded – on the whole – in favour of reason. But emphasis now began to be put on knowledge derived from observation of the material world, rather than a priori theories – a philosophy developed by Francis Bacon (1561–1626), and forming the basis for the empiricism that dominated historical study in the following two centuries. This 'scientific' view of history is most closely associated with the nineteenth-century French philosopher Auguste Comte, who tried to identify broad laws governing human society and history. He called his philosophy 'positivism' to stress its link with 'true' data.

The historian who has come to represent the pursuit of objective truth in history is Leopold von Ranke (1795–1886), thanks to his stated intention to write history *wie es eigentlich gewesen* – as it actually happened. Rows about to what degree this is possible have persisted ever since. Indeed, it was live in Ranke's own day, with British historians such as Thomas Babington Macaulay (1800–1859) and Thomas Carlyle (1795–1881) stressing the literary aspects of their profession; for Macaulay facts were 'but the dross of history'. But it was perhaps the Italian thinker Benedetto Croce (1866–1952) who first consciously addressed the issue, stating that all history was 'contemporary history', in other words was always seen through the eyes of the present. Debate rumbled on. At the beginning of the twentieth century, J.B. Bury declared in his inaugural address at Cambridge University, 'history is a science, no less and no more,' while R.G. Collingwood echoed Croce in *The Idea of History*, published in 1945, which stated: 'History is the re-enactment in the historian's mind of the thought whose history he is studying.' Carr's relativist *What is History?* (1961) insisted that 'the facts of history never come to us "pure", since they do not and cannot exist in a pure form: they are always refracted through the mind of the recorder'. But in 1967, another Cambridge academic, G.R. Elton, argued in *The Practice of History* for the autonomy of history and the importance of the professional historian – 'those who crawl upon the frontiers of knowledge with a magnifying glass'.

Meanwhile, in France, Michel Foucault, Roland Barthes and Jacques Derrida were paving the way for postmodernism, raising questions about links between truth and the power systems that determine it and about the significance of texts. In 1970s America, Hayden White described histories as 'verbal fictions, the contents of which are as much invented as found'. All this hit Britain in the next two decades when Alun Munslow started the journal *Rethinking History*, and Keith Jenkins, in a book of the same title, argued that 'history in the main is what historians make', 'a shifting problematic discourse'. The debate continued with *In Defence of History* (1997) by Richard J. Evans, author of this book's companion article. Evans's book is highly critical of Jenkins and concludes: 'It really happened, and we really can, if we are very scrupulous and careful and self-critical, find out how it happened and reach some tenable, though always less than final conclusions about what it all meant.'

So much for *how* history should be studied. For a long time the idea of *what* it should study had remained fairly constant, with the odd exception of such thinkers as Khaldun and later, in the eighteenth century, Voltaire. If history was to provide some kind of moral or religious guidance and offer examples to follow then surely great events and the great men who took part in them were where it should look. 'Wars, and the administration of public affairs are the principal subjects of history,' wrote Edward Gibbon in the preface to his *Decline and Fall of the Roman Empire* (1776–88). For Ranke, politics and diplomacy were the only places worth looking for his objective facts.

It was Karl Marx (1818–1883) who shifted the emphasis decisively. In the *Communist Manifesto* he stated: 'The history of all

hitherto existing society is the history of class struggles.' His interpretation of history, known as 'historical materialism', argued that
the driving force behind history was satisfying material needs and
that human economic relationships were therefore at its core. This
helped change who and what were viewed as the proper subjects for
historical study. Following Marx's line, ordinary people played an
important role in how societies developed – they too became worth
a look.

Marx was a particular influence on the *Annales* school of historians, based around the journal founded in 1929 by Lucien Febvre
and Marc Bloch in France. They emphasised the importance of
social, economic, cultural, even geographical forces in history and
later of *mentalités* – mental structures. Their aim was for a 'total history', bringing in all aspects of a society. Later *annalistes*, using the
new resources of computerisation, also placed great emphasis on
statistics for exploring such aspects as climate change.

Computers are now changing the study of history in different
ways. Hyperlinks mean the possibility of history without a single
historical voice, making it easier for everyone to become, in some
senses, their own historian. This has contributed to the increasing
popularity of branches of history such as heritage and genealogy,
which are not the preserve of professional historians. It has also
aided globalising and democratising trends in the study of history,
displayed in such works as Daniel Woolf's *The Social Circulation of
the Past: English Historical Culture 1500–1730* (2003), which looks at
how people other than historians influenced history writing in the
past, or Richard Price's *Alabi's World* (1990), which weaves together
the voices of slave descendants, colonial reports and missionary
diaries with his own as a historian.

Postmodernism has not only prompted the tendency for cultural history to replace social and economic analyses as the mainstream of historical study, it has, to some extent, disintegrated the
idea of a mainstream altogether, with many different kinds of history now being practised. Oral history is receiving greater attention,
leading to examination of the role of memory in history. Other ideas
influenced by postmodernism include the concept of history as performance, as described by Greg Dening: 'the effect most worth producing for a writer . . . is a creative reader. We have to stir the
exegete, make the critic, join them to a conversation . . . we need to

perform our texts.' Or history as film. Robert Rosenstone's 1998 *Visions of the Past: The Challenge of Film to Our Idea of History* argues that historical films should not be judged on historical accuracy – the nature of film makes accuracy impossible – but for what they nevertheless reveal about the past. From historical film it is but a short step to television history and the recent cult of celebrity historians. Here, it is not the possibility of many different voices that dominates but the possibility of a single, opinionated one, consciously appealing to the viewer and putting a personal slant of the past.

Views about history have never been straightforward. In *The Nature of History* (1970) Arthur Marwick says that 'the history of historical writing cannot be chopped up into neat compartments . . . there has at all times been a vociferous opposition to whatever orthodoxy has in conventional historiography been regarded as the prevailing one of the time'. More recently, Evans has described the field as a 'palimpsest'. Even for those who believe in the possibility of definitive answers where history is concerned, the question 'What is history?' has usually proved troublesome, but, like those who believe it can never be satisfactorily answered, they are unlikely to stop asking it.

What makes
a great leader

What makes a great leader?

Brendan Simms

Reader in the history of international relations at the University of Cambridge and fellow in history at Peterhouse, Cambridge

Ever since antiquity men have turned to history for lessons in leadership. Things are no different today. At the most mundane level, aspiring business people the world over are increasingly turning to the great leaders of the past for guidance. Self-help manuals with titles such as *Elizabeth I CEO: Strategic Lessons from the Leader who Built an Empire, Nothing to Fear: Lessons in Leadership from FDR* and *Alexander the Great's Art of Strategy: Lessons from the Great Empire Builder* speak for themselves.

In the exalted world of high politics, the search for historical invigoration is even more pronounced. Take, for example, Niall Ferguson's *Empire: How Britain Made the Modern World*, the US edition of which promises 'lessons in global leadership'. Likewise, the strategic historian Eliot Cohen found his tome *Supreme Command: Soldiers, Statesmen and Leadership in Wartime* commended by US President George W. Bush – large numbers of copies were ordered for the White House after 11 September 2001. Cohen's account of the leadership skills of President Abraham Lincoln, Winston Churchill and the first Israeli president, Ben-Gurion, would – it was hoped – inspire similar qualities in Bush Jr as he confronted the challenge of twenty-first-century terrorism.

Of all the exemplars of leadership, Winston Churchill has been the most enduring. The prescience with which he foresaw the emergence of the Nazi threat, the resilience with which he responded to early reverses in the Second World War and the emotional intelligence with which he related to the British people make him an irresistible model for politicians today. It should therefore come as no surprise to find that Prime Minister Tony Blair's strong stance against Saddam Hussein was cast in explicitly Churchillian terms. Indeed, Blair implicitly suggested the comparison himself when he drew a parallel with the 1930s in a remarkable speech before Parliament on the eve of the Iraq War.

There is no doubt that Blair showed historic qualities of leadership throughout the Iraq crisis. Globally, he leveraged an important but modest military contribution and a seat on the United Nations Security Council to help persuade Bush to restart the Middle East peace process and bring the issue of Iraq back to the UN one last time. In Europe, Blair freed Britain from being a minority of one, in a group of three dominated by France and Germany, to lead nine European states more sympathetic to US intentions. Domestically, Blair kept the lid on parliamentary opposition through a combination of arm-twisting, rhetorical sleights of hand and sheer force of argument.

Nor was this the first time that Blair had shown such decisive leadership. It was manifested in Northern Ireland in his decision to enter talks with Sinn Fein without prior decommissioning, and in his persuasion of the Ulster Unionists to keep talking on the basis of promises that were later not so much disregarded as overtaken. The result was the Good Friday Agreement of 1998 at which Blair famously spoke of feeling the 'hand of history' on his shoulder. But perhaps the most remarkable example of Blair's leadership was his role in the defeat of President Slobodan Milošević during the Kosovo War of 1999, when he kept his head while all around were losing theirs. All this contrasted with the timidity of his Conservative predecessor John Major.

To query the comparison with Churchill is therefore not to doubt the prime minister's ability to rise to a challenge similar to that of the 1930s. Nor is it to query whether Blair has Winstonian quantities of charisma. Nor even is it to deny that the prime minister showed Churchillian goodwill in his studied disavowal of triumphalism in victory. The distinction lies elsewhere: Churchill led his people once they had seen that there was no alternative; over Iraq, Blair led the British people, Whitehall and the armed services where they had never intended to go. In that sense, his achievement was the greater; it was certainly quite different. After all, leadership cannot be abstracted from context. As Karl Marx famously reminds us, men may make their own history, but they do not do so in circumstances of their own choosing.

To find a parallel in creatively destructive, unexpected and perhaps unplanned leadership, we must turn to the Prussian and later German chancellor Otto von Bismarck, the architect of German unification in 1871.

At first sight, the comparison seems odd, even perverse. Bismarck was a staunch conservative; Blair is a social democrat. Bismarck saw himself as a conservative realist, a mere 'navigator on the stream of time'; Blair sees himself as a radical reformer: he favours the rhetoric of possibility over that of limitation. Bismarck was a self-conscious apostle of realpolitik; Blair is the avatar of the doctrine of international community by which the world community is obliged to carry out humanitarian interventions, even where these conflict with state sovereignty.

But in terms of leadership, the parallels are intriguing. Both men transcended their origins. Bismarck moved from being a defender of a narrow conservative Prussian aristocratic interest to the hero of the liberal nationalist project, which meant the end of the Prussia he had sworn to defend. Likewise, Blair travelled far from his roots as a campaigner for nuclear disarmament to linchpin of a shaky international coalition to 'disarm' Iraq. Both men looked for support across party lines. Both claimed, not entirely implausibly, to have remained consistent throughout. Neither, however, was ever trusted by his 'core constituency' again. Like many great leaders, both men unsettled their following as much as they inspired it.

Both men had to contend with fractious parliaments and publics. Before German unification, Bismarck was tormented by the liberal majority in the Prussian assembly – the Landtag – which refused to pass his budgets. Blair confronted profound parliamentary scepticism on the wisdom and morality of the invasion of Iraq, and, more generally, hostility on a range of domestic issues, especially taxation and university tuition fees, from a public wary of the costs of messianic visions.

Above all, both men embarked on great integrative projects. Parallels exist between Bismarck uniting Germany, perhaps without at first intending to, and Blair's ambitions to lead early twenty-first-century Europe. For the project of European integration is now at roughly the same stage as that of German unification by 1860. Ever since the customs union – or *Zollverein* – of 1834, economic integration had been proceeding apace; but political unification continued to founder on the objections of smaller German states to surrendering their independence, and especially on the refusal of Austria to allow itself to be sidelined by Prussia and ejected from Germany. What finally persuaded them to pool their sovereignty was the manifest failure of the German Confederation, a loose and congenial political commonwealth, to provide security against suspected French aggression. The confederation fluffed its challenges during the revolution of 1830 and the Rhine crisis of 1840, so Bismarck was later able to sell unity as the only way for southern and western Germany to guard against the pretensions of Napoleon III.

So it is with the European Union. Here, too, the project of economic integration via the single market and single currency is well advanced. Here, too, political and military integration has repeatedly stalled despite sustained efforts: the crises in the former Yugoslavia did not – as the much lampooned foreign minister of Luxembourg suggested – prove the 'Hour of Europe'. The vaunted European defence identity was exposed as the very model of a modern chocolate soldier – swathed in a gaudy multilateralist wrapper, saccharine-sweet on the principles of consensus, but flaky when put to the test. The remedy, the greater defence cooperation announced at St Malo in 1998, simply did not stand up in the confrontations over Iraq.

For Blair to succeed in seizing the initiative in Europe, Parliament and the British people would have to find a way of sanctioning the removal of Saddam Hussein even if no weapons of mass destruction were ever found. He would have to upstage the Franco-German partnership without appearing to be a Trojan horse for the United States. He would have to abandon the battered doctrine of 'pre-emption' and make 'regime change' the cornerstone of a pan-European foreign policy. The next conflict – and there will always be a next one – would have to be waged as a war of European unity.

Such leadership can only be legitimated through success. The Prussian Landtag was awed and beguiled by Bismarck into passing an 'indemnity law', which retrospectively validated his actions. This paved the way for further initiatives culminating in a united Germany in 1871. In the same way, perhaps future attitudes to Blair's leadership will be forgiving enough to allow historians to say that the unification of Europe was brought about not by economic convergence, consensual resolutions and constitutional conventions, but by blood and iron. If so, they may well be reminded of Oliver Cromwell's dictum on leadership: 'He goeth furthest who knows not where he is going.'

Further reading

Eliot Cohen: *Supreme Command: Soldiers, Statesmen and Leadership in Wartime* (Oxford University Press, 2002)

Niall Ferguson: *Empire: How Britain Made the Modern World* (Allen Lane, 2003)

John Kampfner: *Blair's Wars* (Free Press, 2003)

Andrew Rawnsley: *Servants of the People: The Inside Story of New Labour* (Hamish Hamilton, 2000; Penguin, 2001)

A.J.P. Taylor: *Bismarck: The Man and the Statesman* (1955; Sutton Publishing, 2003).

For Otto von Bismarck, the man who united Germany in 1871, great leadership was about little more than 'listening to the rustle of God's cloak' and 'seizing the hem as he passes across the stage of history'. Bismarck's contemporary, Karl Marx, had an even more dismissive view of the impact that individuals' personal qualities can have on history. In his 1852 essay, *The Eighteenth Brumaire of Louis Bonaparte*, Marx mocked Victor Hugo's account of the 1799 French *coup d'état* for elevating Napoleon Bonaparte (Louis Bonaparte's uncle) to the status of a 'great' by 'ascribing to him a personal power of initiative unparalleled in world history'. 'I, on the contrary, demonstrate how the class struggle in France created circumstances and relationships that made it possible for a grotesque mediocrity to play a hero's part,' said Marx.

Many historians have been reluctant even to see history in terms of 'great men', let alone to address the question of what makes a great leader. Leaving such questions to the business gurus and the exploding academic field of leadership studies, they have preferred to focus on the interaction between individuals and their context. In his 1961 *What is History?*, E.H. Carr said: 'Had Bismarck been born in the 18th century . . . he would not have united Germany and might not have been a great man at all.'

Even before Marx, in the era when great men were still placed at the heart of history, thinkers accepted that circumstances played an important role. Edward Gibbon accepted in his monumental *Decline and Fall of the Roman Empire* (1776–88) that 'the genius of Cromwell . . . might now expire in obscurity', because 'times must be suited to extraordinary characters'. Thomas Carlyle, who once proclaimed that 'no sadder proof can be given by a man of his own littleness than disbelief in great men', had to concede that the French Revolution was driven more by social suffering than by any great leader. And the view even has resonance in recent leadership studies. John Adair, appointed the world's first professor of leadership studies in 1978, said: 'It is difficult to be a great leader in Luxembourg in a time of peace.'

But Carr did leave a chink of light for leaders to impose their individual qualities once circumstances had thrust them into greatness. He said that Georg Wilhelm Friedrich Hegel, in his 1821 *Philosophy of Right*, had summed up his view perfectly: 'The great man of the age is the one who can put into words the will of his age, tell his age what its will is, and accomplish it . . . he actualises his age.' Carr explained: 'The view which I would hope to discourage is the view which places great men outside history and sees them as imposing themselves on history by virtue of their greatness . . . But the higher degree of creativity may perhaps be assigned to those great men who, like Cromwell or Lenin, helped mould the forces which carried them to greatness, rather than to those who, like Napoleon or Bismarck, rode to greatness on the back of already existing forces.'

Yet in his 1997 book, *In Defence of History*, Richard J. Evans (see the chapter 'What is history?') argues that Carr still left too little room for the individual and his leadership talents. Under Carr's thesis, Evans says, 'Hitler would have remained a disregarded figure in the lunatic fringe of German politics but for the depression of 1929–33 and the attendant crisis of the Weimar Republic'. Evans says that, on the contrary, once such an individual attains a significant degree of power, then personality traits come into play which may have little or nothing to do with vast impersonal forces, and suggests that Carr was a little too quick to dismiss them.

Those historians and thinkers who have addressed the kind of qualities that enable leaders to mould the social forces around them have diverged little in their views across the centuries. While Niccolò Machiavelli's *The Prince* (1513) has been dismissed as a model of duplicitous and manipulative political manoeuvring, or 'a handbook for gangsters' (rather than great leaders), as Bertrand Russell described it, it has remained one of the most enduring leadership manuals of all time; indeed Napoleon said it was 'the only book worth reading'.

One political skill that Machiavelli highlighted was the need to keep potential enemies and critics close. 'When you see that the adviser thinks more about himself than about you . . . [he] will never be a good adviser . . . The prince should think of the adviser in order to keep him good – honouring him, making him wealthy, putting him in his debt, giving him a share of the honours and the responsibilities – so that the adviser sees that he cannot exist without the prince.' Almost 2,000 years earlier, and across the other side of the world, the Chinese military strategist Sun Tzu had said much the same thing in *The Art of War* – a tract not translated into Machiavelli's language until long after his death. Sun Tzu said that in military strategy, you should always leave an escape route for encircled enemy troops, so they will not be obliged to fight to the death. Keith Grint, in his 1997 book *Leadership*, applied this to modern business leadership: 'If you have not demonstrated magnanimity in victory, if you have prevented them from saving face in defeat, they will surely come looking for revenge.'

Biographers have repeatedly pointed out that successful leaders surround themselves with constructive dissenters and potential challengers. Hugo Young's 1993 biography of Margaret Thatcher, *One of Us*, highlighted her ability to keep the factions of the Conservative Party together and her willingness to keep critics such as Michael Heseltine and Keith Speed in her Cabinet. An ability to listen to dissenting voices is central to the leadership thesis of American political historian Eliot Cohen, expressed in *Supreme Command: Soldiers, Statesmen and Leadership in Wartime* (2002). He stresses that successful wartime leaders listened to the often unpalatable and conflicting views of their military leaders and were 'able to listen to and absorb fresh ideas'.

But Machiavelli also praised ruthlessness, 'for a man who wishes to profess goodness at all times will come to ruin among so many who are not good. Hence it is necessary for a prince who wishes to maintain his position to learn how not to be good.' He said: 'It is much safer to be feared than to be loved when one of the two must be lacking.' This was not a view shared by US President Dwight Eisenhower, who said pulling a piece of string will make it follow you while pushing it will 'get you nowhere at all', but the far more successful Theodore Roosevelt did take it on board. According to him, you go far if you 'carry a big stick'. And Ian Kershaw (see the chapter 'How does personality affect politics?'), a leading authority on Hitler, echoes this. 'Whether it be Hitler's murderous Night of the Long Knives or Harold Macmillan sacking half his cabinet in his own slightly less bloody Night of the Long Knives in 1962, a degree of ruthlessness is essential,' he says.

Also crucial, according to Machiavelli, is image, irrespective of real personality – something that the legions of spin doctors employed by Prime Minister Tony Blair confirm is just as valued today. 'Everyone sees what you seem to be, few touch upon what you are,' Machiavelli advised.

Max Weber (1864–1920), whose essay on the three types of legitimate rule or authority many regard as the unassailable account of personality-based leadership, put image first, too. The German sociologist said that leaders can exercise power in one of only three ways: under legal authority, based on established and accepted laws and procedures; under traditional authority, based on the established 'belief in the sanctity of immemorial traditions' such as patriarchal authority or the divine right of kings; or under charismatic authority, which he suggested was the most important. According to Weber, 'Charisma is a quality of an individual personality by virtue of which he is set apart from ordinary men and treated as endowed with supernatural, superhuman or at least specifically exceptional qualities.' This kind of 'charismatic' authority was epitomised by four times British Prime Minister William Gladstone (1809–1898), who won public opinion at first as 'the people's William' and later as 'the grand old man'.

Central to the charismatic leader's repertoire, alongside personality ticks and props, like Churchill's cigar and V-sign, are the powers to persuade through communication skills, characterised by Roosevelt's 'fireside chats', for example, or Hitler's rally rants. Richard Neustadt put the power of persuasion at the heart of his 1960 book, *Presidential Power* (revised in 1990 as *Presidential Power and the Modern Presidents: The Politics of Leadership from Roosevelt to Reagan*). Populist historian Andrew Roberts cited St Paul's proclamation in the Bible: 'If the trumpet shall give an uncertain sound, who shall prepare himself to the battle?' when he made communication – 'the lexicon of leadership' – the central leadership quality in his book *Hitler and Churchill*. For Roberts, 'the unchanging vernacular' of leadership has endured almost unchanged. 'To read Pericles' Funeral Speech of 431 BC ("Athens crowns her sons"), or John Pym's "The cry of all England" speech of 1642, is to appreciate that the stock of human emotions to which leaders appeal is limited and remarkably constant,' he writes. Hitler and Churchill 'both pillaged that short lexicon in their different ways'.

For Roberts this simple language of leadership could be 'plundered, plagiarised, but above all learned'. Writing 2,000 years earlier, Plato acknowledged in the *Republic* that the training in rhetoric – the art of public speaking – offered by the Sophists and fourth-century BC teacher Isocrates, could help propel people to power. But he argued that this created the dangerous possibility of the wrong leader gaining control at the hands of democracy, or 'the large dangerous animal' of popular opinion. Plato argued that simple learned *expertise* was the only true leadership quality. In his *Republic*, he wrote that leaders who rise through public popularity 'completely fail to understand that any genuine sea-captain has to study the yearly cycle, the season, the heavens, the stars and winds, and everything relevant to the job, if he is to be properly equipped to hold a position of authority in a ship'. Or, as Henry Ford (1863–1947) put it: 'The question who ought to be boss is like as who ought to be the tenor in the quartet. Obviously the man who can sing tenor.'

How does personality affect politics

How does personality
affect politics?

Ian Kershaw
Professor of modern history at the University of Sheffield

? How did Hitler's narcissism influence his dominance of German politics during the Third Reich?
How far was Nazi policy dictated by the obsessive
hatred of Jews that was unquestionably a vital feature of
Hitler's personality? These apparently simple questions demand highly complex answers, even for one of
the most studied individuals in history.

The guessing game about Hitler's personality
and psychological make-up has never ceased since it
began soon after he first attracted attention in the
Munich beer halls. One recent speculation finds the
key in his presumed homosexuality, another in the
syphilis he allegedly contracted from a Viennese
prostitute. Was the young Hitler drawn into the
Viennese gay scene? Or did he frequent brothels? Or
neither? No one ever put him on the couch and asked
him. Had they done so, they would probably not have
lived to tell the tale. So it all remains intellectual
guesswork, prompting the reductionism beloved of
psycho-historians.

Indeed, if we are honest, we have to admit that,
on one of the most important issues affecting Hitler's
personality, we just do not know. It is impossible to be
sure where, how, when and why Hitler acquired such
obsessive hatred of Jews. So it is perhaps best to accept
it as a given and seek to answer the more important
question of how this obsession helped Hitler's rise to
power then translated itself into genocidal policy once
he ruled Germany. But this then turns into a question
ranging far beyond Hitler's personality, which has to be

fitted as *one* strand of a much wider and more complex framework of causation of his extraordinary impact on German politics and the reasons why the Jews of Europe came to be murdered in their millions.

And however much the personality of the individual in this one – self-evidently important – issue needs to be taken into account, no deductions can be drawn from it about the effect of personality on politics generally. Each individual's personality is unique. Even if the psychological and motivational forces that shape a personality could be fully and accurately established, this would have significance only for that singular case, and even then would only be one part of an explanation of the individual's political effectiveness. In fact, as the example of Hitler shows, the psychological underpinnings of political motivation can often be grasped only imperfectly. All that can be said is that where individuals play a significant role in politics, their specific imprint is shaped in part by the traits of their personality – hardly an earth-shattering conclusion.

A more promising approach would be to move away from concentrating directly on 'personality' to consider the related but separable issue of the effect of the individual on the political process, quite specifically upon the shaping of major political change. Here, it is worth bearing in mind Karl Marx's dictum on Louis Bonaparte: 'Men do make their own history, but they do not make it just as they please; they do not make it under circumstances chosen by themselves, but under circumstances directly encountered, given and transmitted from the past.' The maxim can be applied to dictators as well as democrats, to absolute monarchs as well as revolutionary leaders. Take, as an example from a pluralist democracy, Margaret Thatcher, in personality terms the most assertive postwar British prime minister. It would be absurd to deny that she had a substantial effect upon late twentieth-century politics in this country. The single-minded pursuit of objectives – 'the lady's not for turning' – in overriding all opposition, both of organised Labour and of the 'wets' in her own Cabinet, was legendary and is central to her own self-styled historical image, the 'Thatcher Myth'.

It did, of course, demand strong will and great tenacity to combat the then powerful unions, particularly the miners. And Thatcher unquestionably left an indelible personal imprint upon the style of her government – a 'handbagging' has become popular parlance. But, seen in terms of the longer run of British politics and economic development in the second half of the twentieth century, Thatcher's ability in eleven years of rule, backed by huge majorities, to bring about fundamental change seems more limited – shaped, but also constrained, by objective structural determinants which even she was not able to control or master. Given an alternative Conservative prime minister, the confrontation with the unions would certainly have been less brutal. But the unstoppable changes in the world economy – including declining demand for steel and coal, the revolution in information technology, and globalisation – would have necessitated under any government the systematic reorientation of the British economy, which Thatcher at best accelerated by drastic methods. And, for all the emphasis she placed upon radical change, the hallmark of her legislative programme (as of almost all governments this century) was continuity. Most of the legislation she inherited went unrepealed. Thatcher, in other words, had an effect on British politics. But it would be as well not to exaggerate her personal ability to bring about significant long-term change.

The same point could be made of the British prime minister, Tony Blair. What might be said of both is that as 'presidential' styles of running the British government have apparently replaced the role of Cabinet – to my mind, in any case, an exaggerated assertion – external constraints on the room for manoeuvre of British prime ministers have grown, not diminished.

In authoritarian regimes, there are fewer constraints on regime leadership than under pluralist-democratic systems of government. It would be perverse to suggest that an individual dictator does not have a profound influence upon his regime's policy. To try to reduce Hitler to no more than a cipher for the interests of big business always was an absurdity. Under another leader of Germany in the 1930s, it is doubtful whether national assertiveness would have been taken so far that general European war was the consequence, and almost certain that discrimination against Jews would not have led to the 'Final Solution'.

Yet even dictators are not free agents. Here, too, the personal role is conditioned by an array of internal and external determinants that the individual can influence only to a minor degree, if at all. Most authoritarian leaders are bound by the interests of the power groups they represent – normally the army and a ruling, monopoly party. Given the invariably accompanying repression, successful resistance from below is rare. But if the interests of the power elites are not upheld, other contenders for leadership emerge, and a mass basis of support for a new claimant is engineered. The result is usually that either the person of the dictator is changed or the regime is replaced.

In exceptional circumstances, however, usually following a period of most profound crisis or revolutionary upheaval, a dictator is able to build such a level of personalised power that he is able, for a relatively short period, to override the sectional interests of the elites which hoisted him to power, break the constraints that these normally impose, and even to threaten to undermine or destroy those interests. Here, the effect of the individual is indeed extremely far-reaching. But it is usually of fairly short duration – if seemingly endless for those who have to suffer the appalling consequences. The obvious examples are the two most infamous dictators of the twentieth century, Hitler and Stalin.

Hitler, like all modern dictators, ruled by a combination of manipulated acclamation and terrorising repression. But, until the middle of the war, his decisions were not out of step with the interests of the major power elites in Germany. And until the war started to turn sour, he also enjoyed a high level of genuine popularity in Germany, based upon what were widely perceived to be his 'successes' and 'achievements'. This enabled him gradually to establish a personal dominance unusual even for dictators and to break free of the constraints that the traditional power elites might otherwise have imposed. By the time the power elites recognised that Hitler was leading them to national disaster, it was too late. Dissident groups failed to overthrow him from within. Nothing was left but to await the destruction of the regime from outside. When all account is taken of structural determinants in the course of the Third Reich, Hitler's personal imprint upon what happened is undeniable. But that personal role has still to be located in the constellation of forces that created and sustained such a destructive and inhumane regime. Politics, even in the Third Reich, cannot be reduced to the role of the individual.

In Stalin's case, while the personal imprint upon politics is also self-evident, there were alternatives open to the Soviet leadership when Stalin gained power. The path taken through brutal collectivisation was Stalin's choice. And the extreme levels of terror directed at his own people (whereas Hitler's was mainly exported) reflected Stalin's paranoid personality. But the violent nature of Stalin's regime cannot be reduced simply to an expression of the dictator's paranoia. Not only did it mirror the social and political forces that had produced such a monster, the terror was only possible because it accorded with the interests of, and was backed by, the dominant forces within the Communist Party, both at the centre and in the provinces.

However, as terror spawned terror, the party increasingly became little more than a vehicle of the elaborated Stalin personality cult, while the army leadership was decimated in the purges. Stalin, like Hitler, but in this case more through terror and fear than plebiscitary acclamation, had largely freed himself from internal political constraints. The war, in which Stalin (unlike Hitler) gradually acknowledged the need to concede strategic decisions to military professionals, then raised him to a new pedestal of national hero. Until his death in 1953, therefore, the dictator was untouchable, his personal steerage of Soviet politics indisputable.

Whether an internal coup would have been attempted at some point had he lived much longer is purely a matter of speculation. What was remarkable, nonetheless, was the rapidity with which party dominance, undermined while he was alive, reasserted itself as soon as he was dead. The structurally damaging aspects of Stalinism, especially the extreme insecurity under his rule of all echelons of government and administration, were, with remarkable speed, converted into orthodox repressive authoritarianism under party domination. Between Khrushchev and Gorbachev, the leader of the Soviet Union was no dictator in the Stalin mould, but the representative figure of party interests. Dramatic change came under Gorbachev because traditional party interests were no longer compatible with economic realities. Fundamental alteration was recognised as inevitable by parts of the Soviet elite. Once introduced, the change was unstoppable. The system collapsed. The individual, Gorbachev, had been the agent, or catalyst, of change. But his role had been essentially to acknowledge that the impersonal forces demanding change could no longer be held back, Canute style.

These examples suggest a number of generalised hypotheses about the effect of the individual upon politics. Firstly, in pluralist-democratic systems, where political decisions are reached by rational (in an expedient sense) processes of deliberation, the role of even powerful personalities in bringing about major political change is limited and, for the most part, subordinated to the determining influence of wider, more impersonal forces. Secondly, in authoritarian systems, the scope for determining individual influence is much greater – though, here too, more dependent than might at first be thought upon satisfying the interests of the power elites that had created the authoritarian framework of rule in the first place, and subject to external influences and determinants. Ultimately, the individual's role is still circumscribed, though less so than in pluralist systems. Thirdly, some authoritarian systems can nevertheless be described as 'exceptional regimes'. The background here is framed by an extraordinarily far-reaching crisis of legitimacy of the previous system in which the 'heroic' status of the authoritarian leader who emerges from the political turmoil elevates him to a position in which, over time, his personal power becomes a factor of decisive importance, even to the extent that it can begin to erode, or conflict with, powerful sector interests. This 'exceptional rule' can, by definition, last for only a limited period of time before it collapses, is defeated by external forces, is replaced by a more pluralistic system, or subsides into more conventional authoritarianism.

Other than in extraordinary circumstances, therefore, the effect of the individual on politics is – to use an old Marxist term – largely one of 'overdetermination'; that is, of accelerating or retarding to some extent processes which are in the main shaped by impersonal forces. Marx's adage, formulated over a century and a half ago, seems the most appropriate encapsulation of this relationship. So in one thing, at least, Marx was right.

Further reading

Herbert Butterfield: 'The Role of the Individual in History', *History*, 138/9 (1955), pp. 1–17

Peter Clarke: *A Question of Leadership* (Penguin, 1999)
Mary Fulbrook: *Historical Theory* (Routledge, 2002)
Karl Marx: *The Eighteenth Brumaire of Louis Bonaparte* (International Publishers Co., 1963)
Lewis Namier: *Personalities and Powers* (Hamish Hamilton, 1955).

Commentary by Huw Richards
Freelance writer and journalist

Former British Prime Minister David Lloyd George argued that 'a gifted or resolute person has often postponed for centuries a catastrophe which appeared imminent and but for him would have befallen'. Russian writer Leo Tolstoy, on the other hand, believed that 'historical personages are the product of their times, emerging from the connection between contemporary and preceding events' and felt that great men were no more than 'labels giving names to events'. Between these two polar opposites lies the ground on which one of the most basic historical debates is fought, the question of how far individuals can affect history. Are they wholly independent actors, or the prisoners of contexts provided by broad, long-term historical forces? Pitting historical determinism against 'one damn thing after another' and theory against narrative, it is history's version of one of the most elemental of human debates – how far do we have free will?

Personality and politics interact at many levels. The question could embrace the ability of individuals to alter the great sweep of history, or merely the fortunes of a single nation or state. It could take personality to imply individual character quirks and idiosyncrasies, or it might look at one of the most basic of political-science issues: how far an individual candidate or leader can affect the fortunes of a party at local or national level. All historians, even if they never isolate it as an issue, as Herbert Butterfield did in his essay 'The Role of the Individual in History' (1955), must address it.

Yet they do not, whatever some polemical exchanges suggest, tend to the polar extremes illustrated by Lloyd George and Tolstoy. E.H. Carr's *What is History?* (1961) may have cast him as a spokesman for determinism, but in planning for the book's second edition twenty years later he was prepared to accept that Lenin's premature death and Stalin's succession had, in the short term at least, had a significant impact on life in Russia and that 'even if you maintain that in the long run everything would have turned out much the same, there is a short run which is very important and makes a great deal of difference to a great many people'.

Similarly, A.J.P. Taylor may famously have written in 1950

that 'The history of modern Europe can be written in terms of three Titans: Napoleon, Bismarck and Lenin' – Carr noted acidly that he showed no intention of acting on this possibility – but he also quoted approvingly Bismarck's own dictum that 'Man cannot create the current of events. He can only float with it and steer.'

Both Pieter Geyl in *Napoleon For and Against* (1949) and Georges Rudé in *Robespierre* (1975) pointed to the tendency of successive generations of historians to reinterpret both individuals and events in the light of their own age. Rudé noted how the liberal, anticlerical historians of the early Third Republic in France tended to admire Robespierre's great rival Danton, but that growing Marxist influence, the First World War and Russian Revolution in the first decades of the twentieth century produced a swing towards Robespierre.

Another factor is perspective. As Eric Hobsbawm said of the shift by Emmanuel Le Roy Ladurie from the large-scale statistical analysis of *Les Paysans du Languedoc* (1966) to the intensive examination of a single small community in *Montaillou* (1976), it is as legitimate to study history through a microscope as a telescope. And to write biography – in Rudé's words, 'the last redoubt of the cult of personality' is by definition to regard the individual as significant.

Early written history was predominantly biographical – the lives of saints and kings. Ben Pimlott, who wrote best-selling biographies of former British Prime Minister Harold Wilson and Queen Elizabeth II, pointed out that the New Testament is four pieces of biography: the individual forms the whole of the picture. This exclusive emphasis changes once historians start looking to documentary sources in order to reconstruct the past – a process that in Britain has been dated to Gilbert Burnet's *History of the Reformation in England* (1679). It was systematised by the German Leopold von Ranke (1795–1886), founding father of history as a profession. Ranke's exhaustive studies, examining history over long periods, told him that 'every life of historical significance has a determined content', but even his was still history from above, focusing on rulers and their policies.

Britain in particular has a long biographical tradition, centred on the individual political actor. This reached an early apotheosis with Thomas Carlyle, whose books included a life of Cromwell and *Heroes and Hero-Worship* (1841). Victorian politics inspired vast multi-volume biographies of major figures, minutely detailing their public lives, such as John Morley's *Life of Gladstone* (1903), whose modern lineal descendant is Martin Gilbert's exhaustive life of Winston Churchill. It was Benjamin Disraeli who advised reading biography rather than history because biography is 'life without theory'. Emphasis on the individual actor has come naturally to those who see history as closer to literature than social science and are wary of broad theoretical frameworks derived from the techniques and analyses of other disciplines. Geoffrey Elton encapsulated this, emphasising the personal role of Thomas Cromwell in *The Tudor Revolution in Government* (1953) and becoming one of E.H. Carr's most trenchant critics in *The Practice of History* (1967).

Yet even Carlyle saw political causation beyond the great men – citing 'Hunger and nakedness and nightmare oppression lying heavy on 25 million hearts' as the prime cause of the French Revolution. That history might be impelled from below as well as above, by masses as well as individuals, was the contention of Jules Michelet, whose history of the revolution (1847) stated that *'l'acteur principal est le peuple'*. Notable followers of this approach have included George Lefebvre (*La Grande Peur de 1789*, 1932) and, in British history, E.P. Thompson (*The Making of the English Working Class*, 1963).

Approaches treating the individual as prisoner, or at best agent, of broader forces, are most strongly associated with Karl Marx (1818–1883). But his influence is felt well beyond those who would call themselves, or be called, Marxists. It was American historian Arthur Schlesinger Sr who declared in 1928 that the 'Great Man' is 'merely the mechanism through which the Great Many have spoken'.

Meanwhile, the French *annales* school emphasised geography and the long term. Its most famous work, Fernand Braudel's *The Mediterranean and the Mediterranean World in the Age of Phillip II* (1949), has been described as 'concerned to place individuals and events in a wider context, to make them more intelligible at the price of revealing their fundamental lack of importance'.

In the 1950s and 1960s impetus did seem to be with those who stressed the social-science approach. S.T. Bindoff, contributing to a symposium on approaches to history in 1962, noted a tendency to play down the individual. This was particularly strong in countries such as West Germany, where, Richard Evans has noted, historians reacting against the cult of personality under Hitler 'avoided biography and concentrated on writing the history of people in the past mainly as a history of averages, groups and global trends'.

But the traffic was not all one way. Isaiah Berlin responded to E.H. Carr's assault on 'the assumption that the important explanations in history are to be found in the conscious purposes of the dramatis personae' with his *Historical Inevitability* (1954), arguing that man's unique quality was a capacity for choice. External forces did limit individuals, but it was the historian's job to identify how much room they had for manoeuvre and what possible alternative courses of action were available, and judge them accordingly.

In 1979, Lawrence Stone identified a 'Revival of Narrative', arguing that the social sciences had done a great deal for history but had not delivered the grand overarching syntheses they had promised. Certainly, biography has enjoyed a revival since the 1950s.

Moreover, since the early twentieth century, psychology has been persistently significant. Havelock Ellis complained in the 1890s that biographers did not tell him 'a fair proportion of what I wish to know'. This changed in many biographies following Freud, whose proponents included Sir Lewis Namier. He argued in 1955 that 'History is primarily, and to a growing extent, made by man's mind and nature; but his mind does not work with the rationality that was once deemed its noblest attribute'. The analysis of mass psychology that underpinned *La Grande Peur* was now applied to the understanding of individual figures, notably in Max Weber's work on charismatic leadership.

In Britain, while 'high politics' – emphasising the actions of individual politicians rather than wider social forces – has often been identified with the political right, it could be argued that the historiography of the left has benefited more from biography, through works such as David Marquand's *Ramsay McDonald* (1977), Philip Williams's *Hugh Gaitskell* (1979), Ben Pimlott's *Hugh Dalton* (1985) and *Harold Wilson* (1992) and Peter Clarke's *The Cripps Version* (2002). One element in this may be that more of the left's major figures – Dalton, Gaitskell, Richard Crossman, Barbara Castle and Tony Benn among them – were diarists, while the right's diarists such as Henry 'Chips' Channon and Alan Clark tended to be better writers than politicians. Historians like Pimlott increasingly identified diaries as a vital source, contending that biography could and should benefit from the techniques of both literature and social science.

Other writers were unconvinced. Williams's *Gaitskell*, regarded as a magnificent political biography, deliberately steered clear of some aspects of his subject's private life. Ellis would have been happier with Brian Brivati's *Hugh Gaitskell* (1996), which devoted several pages to Gaitskell's affair with Tory hostess Ann Fleming.

Abroad, the reaction to personality cults noted by Evans has led to British rather than native writers producing what are widely recognised as the standard works on the major figures of Spanish and German twentieth-century history – Paul Preston's *Franco* (1993) and the two-volume *Hitler* (1998, 2000) by Ian Kershaw. But what is termed 'the biographical turn' is evidently in force generally, with even German historians now turning to biography – illustrating in particular previously unexplored aspects of Nazism through the lives of those who epitomise them.

Such trends are accentuated by the influence of postmodernism, with its deep distrust of anything that looks like grand theory. Opinion varies sharply over the value of counterfactual volumes in the 'What if ?' vein, with critics arguing that they are essentially entertainments of little more intrinsic historical value than the humorous classic of the genre, James Thurber's 'What if Grant had been Drinking at Appomattox?'. But in their emphasis on the significance of single actions they demonstrate, as much as more conventional biography, a modern appetite for history centred on the individual.

What makes
successful
government

What makes successful government?

Vernon Bogdanor
*Professor of government at Oxford University and
Gresham Professor of Law, Gresham College, London*

? It is easy for government to be successful. Mussolini, so it is said, made the trains run on time, though he appears to have been less good at making war. But any government that can control society and the means of communication has a good chance of proving successful, in the short run at least. The more interesting issue is what makes for successful government in a democracy, a form of polity in which the political leaders depend on public support.

Bob Worcester, founder of MORI, Britain's leading polling organisation, is fond of saying that in a democracy public opinion is king. This is even more so in the era of referendums and focus groups. Still, no country, not even Switzerland, governs entirely through the instruments of direct democracy. Governments everywhere must gauge public opinion for themselves.

But what is public opinion? How are popular attitudes to be distinguished from deeper trends of public sentiment? There can be little doubt, for example, that the British public was solidly behind Neville Chamberlain's policy of appeasement, as indeed the early Gallup polls confirm. This did not stop the public turning on Chamberlain when, in 1940, Britain found itself exposed to a greater danger than it had ever before known. Similarly, before 1982, few British voters held strong views on the Falkland Islands. Nevertheless, had Margaret Thatcher's government been defeated in the attempt to retake them after the Argentine invasion, her government might well have fallen, so great was public outrage against the Argentines.

Successful government, then, does not consist simply in following popular attitudes wherever they may lead. It requires something more. It means discerning those deeper currents of opinion that lie behind the superficial manifestations. It means discerning what Isaiah Berlin once called 'the hoofbeat of history'. Sometimes, that hoofbeat can be heard by political leaders of a quite unintellectual, or even anti-intellectual, cast of mind. Former US Secretary of State George Schultz wrote in his memoirs that he could never understand how Ronald Reagan knew so little but achieved so much. The same could have been said of Franklin Roosevelt.

Yet it is not accidental that so many of the most successful political leaders in modern democracies – in the United States, Theodore Roosevelt and Harry Truman; in Britain, Benjamin Disraeli and Winston Churchill; in France, Charles de Gaulle – have been keen students of history. What they learned from history was not the drawing of superficial analogies – the supposed 'lessons' of Munich or Suez – but rather an understanding of the main political and intellectual forces of the age. For the politician seeking to be a statesman, knowledge of history is priceless.

Knowledge of history can also give us clues as to which types of government are likely to prove successful or unsuccessful. There are in fact three main enemies of successful government. They are ideology, morality and panic.

Ideological government is unlikely to prove successful government, since ideology lies in contradiction to historical understanding. It yields a closed system of thought, rather than a necessary openness to experience. British Labour governments between the years of Clement Attlee and the advent of Tony Blair found themselves victims of what the American political scientist Samuel Beer called 'compulsive ideologism'. This was obviously so in the left wing of the Labour Party which avoided facing up to the realities of the mixed economy and the improvement in working-class living standards in the post-war world. 'The masses,' as Friedrich Engels once said, 'have got damned lethargic after such long prosperity.' But this compulsive ideologism was equally noticeable in the so-called revisionist or Gaitskellite right wing of the party, which was just as preoccupied with discovering the 'true meaning' of socialism. As Beer noted: 'The contestants, whether fundamentalist or revisionist, found themselves in agreement on a basic premise. All accepted the necessity for a social philosophy with programmatic consequences. The opposing sides were at swords' points with regard to their respective ideologies, but they were united in their ideologism.'

It was this fixation on ideology that largely prevented the Labour governments of the Harold Wilson/James Callaghan era in the 1960s and 1970s from coming to grips with economic problems. Labour spent much of its time in opposition in the 1950s discussing the futile question of whether it should 'accept' the mixed economy. It failed to consider the real question of how a mixed economy should be successfully managed. The ideologies of both left and right were like rigid searchlights. In focusing on the problems of yesterday, they turned away from the more difficult challenges of the contemporary world.

Labour had a much better chance of success following the removal in 1995, under Blair's leadership, of Clause 4 of its constitution, advocating nationalisation of the means of production, distribution and exchange, which allowed it to develop into a practical social democratic party on the Continental model. But to govern successfully it is not enough for a leader to lead. He must also find followers who will follow.

Just as a government that seeks to create a new heaven on earth is unlikely to prove successful, nor will a government that imposes its own values upon society. The most striking example of the failure of moralism in government is the attempt to prohibit alcohol in the

United States in the 1920s. Prohibition was characterised by Herbert Hoover, before becoming president in 1929, as 'a great social and economic experiment, noble in motive and far-reaching in purpose'. Yet, far from curing the evils of alcoholism, it encouraged them, since many who had previously been temperate in their habits began to imbibe freely in protest against the invasion of their 'personal liberty' by the law. They demanded more liquor, not less; and, as the American historian of the period John D. Hicks wryly commented, 'private enterprise, although in this instance unassisted by the law, never showed greater efficiency in meeting a consumer demand'. The outcome was not temperance, but bootlegging, and the growth of private armies of gunmen and thugs of whom Al Capone was the most notorious, though by no means the only, example.

Successful government, then, is generally non-ideological government. It is also likely to be limited government rather than hyperactive government. In 1993, Anthony King, a political scientist at Essex University, asked in the *Daily Telegraph*, 'Will the Honourable Action Men please sit down at once?' He was referring primarily to the justly forgotten Tory minister, John Patten, and his education bill of that year, to which the government had added 278 amendments during the House of Commons committee stage, a further 78 during the report stage, 258 during the House of Lords committee stage, 296 on report and 71 at the third reading. Did any of this make the slightest difference to educational achievement? Almost certainly not. We were governed, King complained, 'by an entire tribe of hyperactive children'. Hyperactive governments are prone, moreover, to panic – Kenneth Baker's Dangerous Dogs Act of 1991 and Thatcher's poll tax being striking examples. Much hyperactive government, however, occurs during the first phase of a government's term of office, as with Wilson in 1964, Ted Heath in 1970 and Thatcher in 1979. Whatever the merits of Franklin D. Roosevelt's hundred days in 1933, its repetition by less distinguished practitioners has led only to disaster.

A successful government, it may be thought, leaves a country feeling happier. By that criterion, the peacetime administrations of Churchill and Dwight Eisenhower were successful governments. Yet both, in pandering to the immediate wishes of voters, ignored more serious problems – Churchill failed to develop a sound European strategy while Eisenhower refused to confront McCarthyism or segregation, leaving, in each case, difficult legacies for their successors.

Successful government involves confronting the problems of the future, not those of the past. At the beginning of the last century, Arthur Balfour, though prime minister of a decaying government, established a modern structure for secondary education, machinery for the organisation of defence, and ended Britain's splendid isolation. John Major, an equally undervalued prime minister, who also had to face a withdrawing tide, ensured, through negotiation at Maastricht and skilful parliamentary manoeuvring at Westminster, that Britain remained in the European Union. Moreover, he introduced into the public services many of the techniques and disciplines of the private sector, believing, by contrast with Thatcher, that the public sector did not have to be equated with the second-rate. It is thanks to him that we at least know whether or not the trains are running on time. Posterity will be kinder to Major than his contemporaries have been.

Successful government, then, is government aware of its limitations, quiet government, government by men and women with a highly developed sense of history. The trouble is that successful government, as nineteenth-century journalist Walter Bagehot well knew, is almost always dull government. Those who seek excitement will have to find other fields for exercising their talents.

Further reading

Samuel Beer: *Modern British Politics* (Faber, 1965);
   Britain Against Itself (Faber, 1982)
James MacGregor Burns: *Roosevelt, The Lion and
   the Fox* (Secker & Warburg, 1956); *Leadership*
   (Harper & Row, 1978)
David Butler, Andrew Adonis and Tony Travers:
   *Failure in British Government: The Politics of the
   Poll Tax* (Oxford University Press, 1994)
William Harbaugh: *The Life and Times of Theodore
   Roosevelt* (Oxford University Press, 1975)
Roy Jenkins: *Churchill* (Macmillan, 2001)
Anthony Seldon (ed.): *The Blair Effect* (Little,
   Brown, 2001)
Robert Worcester: *British Public Opinion* (Black-
   well, 1991).

Commentary by Huw Richards
Freelance writer and journalist

'The problem of just what was meant by "a good government" lay at the very heart of political theory. Perhaps it always does.' So wrote historian David Thomson in a short study of the thought of Jean-Jacques Rousseau, written in 1966.

Thomson was looking back over two centuries to Rousseau's era. But few historians or political theorists today would differ from Thomson's viewpoint. No matter what your criterion – whether 'good' or 'effective' or 'successful' government – judgement is almost unavoidably subjective. Ask the most rigorous British observer to rank the administrations of Herbert Asquith, Clement Attlee, Winston Churchill, Anthony Eden, Harold Macmillan or Margaret Thatcher, or get their US counterpart to perform a parallel exercise on the presidencies of Franklin Roosevelt, Dwight Eisenhower, Ronald Reagan and Bill Clinton, and the outcome is likely to tell you more about them than about those governments. As Joseph Nye, founding father of Harvard's Visions of Governance project, the most extensive contemporary study of government, wrote in 1997: 'Purely neutral government is impossible, because citizens want some discussion of what is good.'

The question of what makes good government has been one for the theorists, always vulnerable to the charge laid by the reliably caustic Walter Bagehot in 1867: 'An observer who looks at the living reality will wonder at the contrast to the paper description.' It also cuts across the, in any case ill-defined, border between history and political science. Political science, with its more theoretical bent, has tended to approach it more directly, while the historiography of it is limited, addressed more through implication than frontal assault.

Government's most assiduous recent chronicler, S.E. Finer, author of a compendious three-volume *History of Government* (1997), pointed out in 1970: 'The study of comparative government is as old as Plato and Aristotle but, as its history has shown, is so enormously complicated that its findings and even its basic typology are still fluid.' He also noted that conceptions, expectations and models of government had changed dramatically over time. While dating the earliest forms of government to Sumeria between 3500 and 3200 BC, he also quoted approvingly Jean Dunbabin's comment, in her 1985 study of medieval France, that 'Nobody was governed before the late 19th century. It would certainly be foolish to maintain that either royal or princely government in the 12th century operated according to fixed rules or over all the inhabitants of a fixed area.'

Finer defined five characteristics of a state: a territorially defined population recognising a common authority; specialist bureaucratic and military personnel; recognition as sovereign by other states; a self-conscious common identity; and a population participating in the distribution and sharing of duties and benefits. He noted that both self-conscious identity – which he reckoned emerged in England in the thirteenth century, France two to three hundred years later and Spain as late as the eighteenth century – and popular participation, emerged much later than the other characteristics.

In addition, he noted four essential activities: defence, which he characterised as 'primordial' in that a polity that cannot defend itself has by definition failed; law, order and justice; taxation, although he noted that the Holy Roman Empire had no central treasury or chancery; and the 'highly subjective territory' of public works and welfare.

In analysing change, Finer noted that, until comparatively recently, states were regarded as the property of a ruler chosen by divine right. On this basis, the 1655 claim by Louis XIV of France, '*L'État c'est moi*', generally cited as evidence of vaingloriousness, was also a realistic statement of fact. Finer also pointed out that while the Athens of Plato and Aristotle has been regarded as the starting point of political development, the autocratic militarism of Sparta provided the dominant form of government in the West until the late eighteenth century, with individuals much more likely to be subjects than citizens.

The most prominent thinkers on government have been products of their times. Italy's fratricidal wars informed the subtle mind of Niccolò Machiavelli (1469–1527), whose enduring appeal rests on tough-minded realpolitik – recommending, for instance, 'Men should be either treated generously or else destroyed, because they take revenge for slight injuries, for heavy ones they cannot' – and an elegantly epigrammatic style. He argued for the fundamental importance of military strength ('where there are good arms, good laws invariably follow') and for the supremacy of *raison d'état* ('putting aside every other consideration one ought to follow to the end whatever will save the life of the state and preserve its freedom').

Similarly, the belief of Thomas Hobbes (1588–1679) in the right of the state to impose order so as to curb man's inherently aggressive nature – the alternative being a state of nature in which life was, in his most famed phrase 'nasty, brutish and short' – doubtless owed something to the civil war concluded only two years before the publication of his major work *Leviathan*.

John Locke (1632–1704), epitomising an era which deposed both Charles I and his son James II, devised both a fatal challenge to the doctrine of divine right and one of the basic criteria for defining unsuccessful government – almost invariably more readily discernible than the successful variety. He developed the concept of consent on the basis of contract between ruler and ruled, arguing that 'inconstant, uncertain, unknown and arbitrary government' forfeited consent.

Much subsequent thought was devoted to the question of consent and legitimacy, the ideas espoused by thinkers such as Rousseau and Thomas Paine (1737–1809) reaching a logical conclusion in France's Declaration of the Rights of Man and of the Citizen of 1789: 'Sovereignty resides in the people; it is one and indivisible, imprescriptible and inalienable.'

Neither Paine nor Rousseau, both concerned with human and property rights, intended some of the consequences that flowed from an indivisible concept of property. Many leading nineteenth-century thinkers devoted themselves to the balance between individual and collective rights. Benjamin Constant (1767–1830) argued that 'there is a part of human life which necessarily remains individual and independent, and has the right to stand outside social control', while Jeremy Bentham (1748–1832), best remembered for his proposition that policy should serve 'the greatest good of the greatest number', argued that governments needed to create 'continuity and predictability', enabling their citizens to 'form a general plan of conduct'.

Finer argues that the decisive development for modern government was industrialisation, which transformed its income-generating and -collecting potential, its powers of supervision and surveillance, and created an industrial working class whose demands created pressure for greater intervention in economic and social policy.

While the social democratic parties that grew out of this process were often Marxist in rhetoric, in practice they tended to be followers of Eduard Bernstein, who argued forcibly in the 1890s that the German Social Democratic Party could best achieve its aims by working within existing political structures and, where necessary, cooperation with middle-class liberals.

While there is a long tradition of left-liberal anti-statism – Paine described government as 'a necessary evil' – most resistance to the extension of governmental activity has tended, in English-speaking nations at least, to come from the right.

Such resistance has often been informed by pessimism. Legal academic and writer A.V. Dicey (1835–1922) asserted that 'The beneficial effect of state intervention . . . is direct, immediate and, so to speak, visible while its evil effects are gradual and indirect and lie out of sight . . . Hence the majority of mankind must almost of necessity look with undue favour upon government intervention.'

But then conservative objections to greater intervention do not run across the board. Gary Owen, writing in one of the Harvard project's publications, noted: 'Large numbers have yearned for lower taxes and, in the abstract, less government spending. Yet, through it all, most people have had no trouble thinking of things they would like the federal government to do. The wish list of programmes and services is long and growing.' It was the Italian political philosopher Gaetano Mosca who identified, in 1936, the key to success as the 'political formula', an idea that must 'correspond with the mentality of the age and with the most widely shared sentiments of a people'.

Universal suffrage in Britain brought with it an age that broadly accepted the view expressed by William Beveridge in 1942 that 'The object of government in peace and war is not the glory of rulers or of races, but the happiness of the common man', even if there was wide disagreement on the measures by which this was to be achieved. Hence the expansion of social welfare programmes following the Second World War, and also of political priorities most crisply expressed in the 'It's the economy, stupid' catchphrase used by the successful Clinton presidential campaign of 1992. However anti-government their ideology, conservative politicians have accepted that economic and social welfare is the central concern of politics.

But these developments have been accompanied, particularly in the US, by declining faith in the efficacy of government. Management thinker Peter Drucker argued in 1969 that 'the greatest factor in the disenchantment with government is that government has not performed', a view essentially endorsed in David Osborne and Ted Gaebler's *Reinventing Government* (1992), an influential text for market-minded centre-left politicians such as Al Gore and Tony Blair. Robert Putnam, author of *Bowling Alone: The Collapse and Revival of American Community* (2000), describes the problem as 'a compound of expectations and actual performance'.

Derek Bok, president of Harvard for twenty years until 1991, has concluded that the US has probably not been as well run as other 'leading democracies' since 1960, but his rider to this underlines the continuing subjectivity of the issue: 'To someone who feels that economic growth or poverty and social justice matter more than anything else, it may appear that the country has gone into decline since the 1970s. Conversely, to those who feel especially strongly about the environment, crime, or personal responsibility, America will seem to be doing somewhat better than in the early 1970s, but not as well as it should.'

Successful government, in other words, is in the eye of the beholder. And as the writers of that most penetrating study of government, *Yes Minister*, might have observed, the invariable problem with beholders is that 'I am principled, you are an ideologue, he is a mindless fanatic.'

Why do
empires rise

Why do empires rise?

Richard Drayton
*Senior lecturer in imperial and extra-European history since 1500
at the University of Cambridge*

All empires are expressions of inequality hidden
behind a mask of community. By 'empire' we may
mean something inclusive, a space of shared
peace, sovereignty or rights. Thus in 1533 Henry VIII's
law proclaimed, justifying his pre-eminence over the
English Church, that 'this realm of England is an
empire'. Or we may mean, as we have increasingly
done over the past two centuries, a system through
which a core population dominates a periphery, as
Athens presided over the Delian League, and as the
United States dominates, in different ways, places such
as Haiti or 'allies' such as Britain. A given system will
usually meet both criteria, depending on whether you
look out from the centre or inwards, meaning different
things to the dominant castes on the one hand, and to
those who hew wood or sugar cane and gather water or
oil on the other. In both cases there is a myth of shared
virtue, usually for the consumption of the empire's
elites, but one that may also attract those peripheral collaborators without whom no expansion is possible.
That idea of community is usually proclaimed by those
at the surface of imperial advance: as Spain's *conquista-
dores* burned Arawak villages they carried the cross;
today we drop cluster bombs, murder civilians and tor-
ture prisoners of war in the name of democracy and
human rights.

The essential kind of inequality underlying all
empires is access to violence. At the Roman origin of the
word, the 'imperator' was the military leader, whose
capacity to extract consent was the premise of the

system. Empires, in the sense of a kingdom or a state, begin in the subordination of one community to a power that has the monopoly on legitimate violence within a frontier. Imperial systems grow rapidly at those moments when one community acquires particularly efficient tools or techniques for waging war, and can then include its neighbours into its territory, or subordinate distant peoples. By inventing the modern stirrup, the Mongols were able to fight with both hands, and to dominate Eurasia. Roads and military organisation gave Incas supremacy in the Andes. Breakthroughs in maritime skill and artillery allowed the Portuguese, Dutch, English and French to muscle in on the trade of Africa and Asia after 1500. The classic 'high imperialism' of the late nineteenth century depended directly on the weapons end of the Industrial Revolution, which gave Europeans those repeating rifles and machine guns that allowed them to command the interior of Africa (and indeed of North and South America) for the first time. The latest predatory phase of the American empire, with its ambitions for 'full-spectrum dominance', is essentially a consequence of how satellite and electronic technologies opened up a new arms gap in the late twentieth century.

Why does efficiency in making violence so often turn into a programme of subordinating others? For the optimistic historian and economist Joseph Schumpeter (1883–1950), modern imperialism was only an atavism, the last expression of a medieval warrior aristocracy, soon to be swept away by the peace-loving cosmopolitanism of capitalism. I see it as a more ancient, and so far more enduring, perversion of the human will for survival. We are driven as animals to reproduce and to secure the means of life for our kin. We have long taken the short cut to survival by seizing resources from those we perceive as not like us, and therefore not deserving of equal treatment. Leviticus XXV put the matter frankly: 'the heathen that are round about you' would be the servants of the

Big Questions in History

Hebrews, but 'over your brethren . . . ye shall not rule one over another with rigour'. Or as Prime Minister Tony Blair's confidant Robert Cooper, a senior British diplomat, put it in 2002: 'The challenge to the post-modern world is to get used to the idea of double standards. Among ourselves, we operate on the basis of laws . . . But when dealing with [others], we need to revert to the rougher methods of an earlier era – force, pre-emptive attack, deception, whatever is necessary.' Panic about scarcity or security, channelled through a racial or cultural idea of self and other, has generated over millennia that combination of ruthlessness, greed, self-righteousness and hypocrisy of which every empire is an expression.

A polity's will for power beyond its frontiers grows relative to its appetite for foreign resources. These may include fertile land for settlement (if you are willing to do a little 'ethnic cleansing', as were British settlers in North America and Australia), slave or cheap labour (which might include fertile women), minerals, plunder (either just seizing gems and *objets d'art*, or imposing a tax regime, as did the British in India and the Germans in France), control of the supply of exotic commodities or of markets for exports. The demand for these things, and thus the lunge outwards of Vikings, or Spanish hidalgos, or Zulus, may be the expression of some new environmental pressures, population surges, agrarian crises, ages of ice or drought. The taste for luxuries may, quite independently, impel further aggression. But beyond material advantage, empires also offer symbolic and psychological rewards. Expansion gives the officer class of a society a space in which to exhibit its right to lead, while the men and women who rise to political power often seek exotic theatres in which to swagger. Foreign adventures are sought for their political value, for wars easily generate a patriotic stupor: the *Führer* becomes an adored patriarch, and dissent is silenced as opposition to any elite interest becomes cast as taking the side of the foreigner. Empire, in any event, eases domestic social tensions, as subordinate groups at home are appeased by the idea that, relative to others, they are the master class.

The experiences of violence and inequality generate, in themselves, a terrible momentum. '*Proprium humani ingenii est odisse quem laeseris*,' wrote Tacitus – 'It is in the nature of men to hate those whom we hurt' – to which he might have added, to imitate those who hurt us. The planning, justification and execution of that brutality, which is the basis of each empire, lead themselves to a hardening of racisms and a decay of compassion. The ability to cause pain and death to people who are unable to respond in kind, encourages the powerful to see themselves as different in kind from the others, and becomes part of their identity. A cycle begins: it is no longer enough to be rich and safe at home; the ambition for an extrovert power, which demonstrates its virtue through war, is awakened. This taste for blood is harder to lose than colonies, as dangerous myths about Britain's need to 'punch above its weight in the world' have recently demonstrated. Imperial tradition is a hardy weed that plants roots deeply in a culture, and takes hold easily into the cultures of those who collaborate with, and even those subordinated to, an empire. The seed of Rome is alive in all Western imperialisms, while post-colonial elites, such as in nineteenth-century Latin America or in twentieth-century India, often extend to their more marginal compatriots the authoritarian paternalism of the old regime. In time, the brutalised may become the brutalisers, and nations that began in an experience of oppression, or a war of liberation against colonial tyranny, may export a parasitic despotism.

Empires do not live by violence alone, however, they need equally the idea of community: the myth of some universal interest of which the imperial power is the vanguard. At its simplest, the predators may identify their own community's happiness as a supreme end, relative to which others' misery is insignificant. Power, and the affluence which plunder makes possible at the imperial centre, then comes in a circular way to justify the idealistic violence which keeps expansion growing. They may confuse their own temporary advantages with the idea that they have been divinely elected to dominion over exotic lands or peoples. Religious arrogance is then often translated into the faith that the empire's laws, manners and styles of politics or economy are the best possible. Peripheral people become, at a stroke, Rudyard Kipling's 'half devil and half child', the stubborn and backward who need to be guided by a strong hand towards progress. Those who do not yield to the natural superiority of Jehovah, or Roman law, or Jesus Christ, or Westminster-style parliaments, or privatisation – those, in other words, who refuse to give their resources and labour freely, and to pray or play like their overlords – deserve to be broken. The most successful empires, however, will also bestow, as Edward Gibbon wrote of Rome, 'the freedom of the city . . . on all the gods of mankind', their flexibility allowing the energy of the conquered to be absorbed and harnessed in the arts of war or peace.

At some point, internal contradictions within imperial universalism may cause a moral crisis. People start to believe in its mask, and to demand the same treatment for metropolitan and exotic peoples. But this in itself may generate new imperial causes, as the idea of the 'rights of man' propelled French Revolutionary conquests across Europe in the 1790s, and as Victorian anti-slavery after 1850 turned African kingdoms, which British slave traders had made rich and strong circa 1750, into objects of conquest. The myth of an emancipatory imperialism, of conquest as liberation, that we come, in the boast of nineteenth-century British Prime Minister Lord Palmerston, 'not to enslave but to set free', has proved a potent ideological talisman. It has lent comfort, at different moments, to those who bore the swastika into the Sudetenland, the hammer and sickle into Poland, and the Union Jack and Stars and Stripes into Iraq. Violent is their awakening from this delusion.

Further reading

C.A. Bayly: *The Birth of the Modern World, 1780–1914* (Blackwell, 2004)

C. Cipolla: *Guns, Sails and Empires: Technological Innovation and the Early Phases of European Expansion, 1400–1700* (Sunflower University Press, 1996)

R. Drayton: *Nature's Government: Science, Imperial Britain and the 'Improvement' of the World* (Yale University Press, 2000)

D. Headrick: *The Tools of Empire: Technology and European Imperialism in the Nineteenth Century* (Oxford University Press, 1981).

Commentary by Anna Fazackerley
Writer on the Times Higher Education Supplement

Julius Caesar, the military dictator whose name was adopted by a long line of Roman emperors, summed it up simply in 47 BC: *'veni, vidi, vici'* ('I came, I saw, I conquered'). Yet the debate about why empires rise has been running ever since. And as controversy rages about whether we are entering a new imperial age, it shows little sign of stopping.

Linda Colley, author of *Captives: Britain, Empire and the World 1600–1850* (2002) has observed that the Roman Empire served both as a source of inspiration for subsequent Western empires and helped legitimise them: Napoleon's decision to call himself emperor and adopt the eagle as his emblem is just one example of the way Roman imagery has crept into the worldwide imperial picture, she says. Similarly, the early insights of Roman historians into empire have influenced writers through the ages.

Although it makes few moral judgements, Suetonius's biography *De vita caesarum* (translated as *The Twelve Caesars*), written in the second century, contains numerous examples of the Roman Empire as a civilising and humane force. But it is equally littered with descriptions of alarming and sometimes absurd brutality. How could the *imperator* Tiberius, who executed anyone who dared to enter a lavatory or brothel carrying a coin bearing the head of his predecessor Augustus, be seen as a good example to follow? Tacitus, who served in the most senior administrative posts under the early empire, also filled his *Annals* and *Histories* – accounts of the first-century Roman Empire – with tales of the corruption and tyranny of imperial rule.

Edward Gibbon, whose *Decline and Fall of the Roman Empire* (1776–88) recalled Tacitus' historical style, captured the essential paradox facing those who sought to emulate the Roman experience. For Gibbon, the military empire of Rome was 'the most civilised portion of mankind', with frontiers 'guarded by ancient renown and disciplined valour'. But success led to decadence and tyranny, and ultimately it fell. In his eyes – and those of many who followed him – any consideration of the ascent is coloured by an awareness of the decline. Many modern historians, too, are keen to emphasise that, contrary to popular belief, empires have not been straightforwardly good or bad, and that our response to them must be correspondingly complex.

So must consideration of why empires rise. Expansion of an empire might not always be a deliberate, well-planned process. Sir John Seeley, who trumpeted the evolution of the British Empire as 'the great fact of modern British history' in his 1884 book *Expansion of England*, also admitted that the growth of the empire was somewhat accidental, suggesting, 'We seem to have conquered and peopled half the world in a fit of absence of mind.' Such lack of intention has been applied to other empires. Hugh Thomas, author of *Rivers of Gold: The Rise of the Spanish Empire* (2004), has suggested that Columbus founded Navidad, the first city in the Spanish Empire, because one of his ships was wrecked nearby and he did not have enough space in his other ships to carry home those who had settled there. This was hardly a strategic beginning.

Many historians and economists have identified commerce as one of the driving forces of empire, suggesting – put simply – that the desire for sugar led to British plantations in the Caribbean, and that the Romans conquered Egypt because they wanted grain. In *Wealth of Nations* (1776), Adam Smith argued that commerce alone was 'the grand panacea' and that British trade – and with it British civilisation – could spread across the world without the need for imperial structures or violence.

This is not to say that scholars have approved of imperialism as an economic decision. The economist John Hobson's essay on imperialism, published in 1902, established a new model of criticism about the economics of empire that was closely followed in much of the socialist writing thereafter. Hobson described the rise of empire as an imprudent answer to the problem of surplus capital. Nations have a straight choice, he said, either to concentrate on the very best political and economic management of their own lands, or 'to spread their power and energy over the whole earth, tempted by the speculative value or the quick profits of some new market, or else by mere greed of territorial acquisition'. According to his model, the only way of preventing imperialism was to strip the elite who benefit from it of their surplus revenues.

This view of empire building fed into Lenin's First World War pamphlet, *Imperialism, the Highest Stage of Capitalism*, written in

Big Questions in History

1916. Here he describes imperialism as the inevitable – and unpalatable – end result of 'the monopoly stage' of capitalism. He lists the components of this 'parasitic capitalism' as: 'monopolies, oligarchy, the striving for domination and not for freedom, the exploitation of an increasing number of small or weak nations by a handful of the richest or most powerful nations'.

Few have time for Lenin's argument now. Indeed, study of the economics of empire has drifted out of vogue in the last two decades, although a handful of historians are still determinedly trying to answer economic questions. Niall Ferguson presents a cost-benefit analysis of the British Empire in his 2003 book, *Empire: How Britain Made the Modern World*, which controversially concludes that the British Empire was, on balance, a good thing. Yes, he concedes, slavery, racial discrimination and brutal response to insurrection were abhorrent. But the free movement of goods, capital and labour, as well as the imposition of law, order and governance across the world were unparalleled triumphs.

To the consternation of some traditionalists, the field of imperialism has changed dramatically in the past twenty years, with discussions of political and economic domination being largely replaced by considerations of cultural identity. At the core of this is an assumption that domination is part of a received mindset, such as the belief (upheld by both the rulers and those they ruled) that some people are civilised while others are savage and need saving. This movement can be traced back to Edward Said. In *Orientalism* (1978), he strove to divert attention away from the well-documented white powerful people and towards the experiences of the colonial natives – introducing the forgotten voice of the 'other' to imperial history.

Implicit within much of this new cultural interpretation of the rise of empire is the assumption that existing representations of these 'others' are distorted by an imperial view of the world, and need to be reworked. The business of recovering what these people really thought and how they saw themselves has brought a diverse range of different academic disciplines into the study of imperial history. It now embraces gender and race studies, literary criticism, art history and even anthropology.

But recently some historians have tried to steer the imperial debate back to Britain. Colley has taken issue with the assumption that the only forgotten voices in the imperial story are non-white ones. In *Captives*, she looks at the beginning of the British Empire – a time when Britain was smaller and more vulnerable – and examines the imperial experience from the perspective of non-powerful British players, from soldiers and sailors to traders and settlers. David Cannadine defiantly turned his back on the post-Said preoccupation with race in *Ornamentalism: How the British saw their Empire* (2001). Rather unfashionably, this examines the world view and social presuppositions of the British men who dominated and ruled the empire. According to Cannadine, the ornamentalism that held the empire up was 'hierarchy made visible'. He says: 'Chivalry and ceremony, monarchy and majesty, were the means by which this vast world was brought together, interconnected, unified and sacralized.'

While much recent imperial history has been concerned with looking closely at particular people or a particular time, many historians agree that the way forward for the subject is for perspectives to get bigger. If empire is a recurring phenomenon then it makes sense to compare different imperial powers. Some have already embarked on this path. C.A. Bayly's *The Birth of the Modern World 1780–1914* (2004) provides a sweeping insight into how different empires changed the political map. And Dominic Lieven's *Empire: The Russian Empire and its Rivals* (2001) uses his specialist subject, the tsarist and Soviet empires of Russia, to examine how geography, ideology, culture and politics shape empires more generally.

Meanwhile, imperial history has been hijacked to address a more topical political question. Is a new empire – the American Empire – rising? US Defence Secretary Donald Rumsfeld said categorically: 'We don't do empire.' But many remain unconvinced. The prolific American journalist Tom Wolfe is one of those to liken America to Rome under Julius Caesar, describing it as 'the mightiest power on earth'. And Ferguson, author of a new book on the subject, *Colossus*, has argued that with 750 military bases in three-quarters of the countries on earth America cannot be regarded as anything other than imperial (though he maintains that this need not be a bad thing).

Whatever the truth of such comments – and doubtless the debate will continue – there is no guaranteeing that the US will ever admit imperial ambitions. After all, as historian Eric Hobsbawm pointed out in his 1987 book *The Age of Empire 1875–1914*, states have often chosen to portray imperialism as something nasty done by other nations, and entirely different from their own expansion of power. Perhaps the one thing that is certain is that these debates will add further to the enrichment and complexity of the study of imperial history.

Why do revolutions happen

Why do revolutions happen?

Fred Halliday

Professor of international relations at the London School of Economics

? What causes revolution is one of the most important historical questions, for two reasons: first, because of the impact on the modern world, in every continent, of revolutions themselves; second, because analysis of the causes of revolution poses methodological and theoretical questions that are central not just to social science and history, but to analysis of modern society and where it is going.

Over the centuries, the question has provoked debates not only among historians and social scientists, but also among participants: those seeking to legitimate revolutions attribute them to deep and irresolvable factors, be they internal or external, while those opposed to rebellion tend to cite immediate political or personal factors, without legitimacy or inevitability. But many of these analyses face the same problems. First, analysts of revolutions tend to operate with a limited, bounded, sense of national political social systems – an England, France or China – and fail adequately to see how individual upheavals are part of a broader context, an international civil war. Second, the recent trend in social science and historical sociology has been to downplay the importance of ideas, beliefs and ideologies in animating both leaders and led; it seems to have come as a surprise to historians of the cold war working on recently opened Soviet archives that Lenin, Stalin and others actually believed in some of what they said. Finally, we need to pay more attention to the actions of leaders, without whom long maturing crises might never have taken the form they did.

It is also worth recalling, in these times of global triumphalism, that periods of upheaval are not aberrant or accidental but are a central feature of the shaping of the modern world. Political theorist Hannah Arendt once observed that the twentieth century, the bloodiest and most rapidly changing epoch in human history, was made by wars and revolutions. If the First and Second World Wars, and the ensuing cold war, did much to shape that age, revolutions – mass political and social upheavals that overthrew states and sought to establish new domestic and international orders – were equally important.

The First World War was preceded, and to a considerable degree precipitated, by revolutions in Russia, Persia, Turkey, Mexico and China, and was followed by the Bolshevik seizure of power, the consequences of which were to last until 1991. The Second World War was followed by the communist seizure of power in China, the imposition of revolutionary change from above in Eastern Europe, and the rise of revolutionary nationalism in Vietnam. The path of the cold war was also marked by a variety of revolutions: orthodox communists in Indochina; radical nationalists in Algeria, Cuba, Angola, Mozambique and Nicaragua; military radicalism in Egypt and Ethiopia; and, finally, a strange pair of contrasted, but adjacent, extremes, the seizure of power by an ultra-dogmatic Communist Party in Afghanistan in 1978, and the mass upsurge of the Islamic revolution in Iran a few months later. It can also be argued that, despite their peaceful nature, the mass movements that overthrew the Communist Parties of Eastern Europe in 1989, and which thereby hastened the collapse of the USSR, were revolutionary in the degree of political, social and economic change they envisaged, and later achieved.

This central role of revolution in modern international history, as well as in that of the individual countries concerned, applies not only to the twentieth century but to preceding centuries as well: the seventeenth century was marked by two major upheavals of a political, economic and ideological kind, the 'Revolt of the Netherlands' (1566–1609) and the event euphemistically referred to as the 'English Civil War' (1642–9), while the eighteenth was marked by the American Revolution (1776–83), and then the most influential and paradigmatic of all, the French (1789). The Europe of the nineteenth century was shaped by the outcome of the revolutions of 1848. Varied as they were in national character and context and in ideological import, as well as in outcome, this not very large but nonetheless immensely significant and comparable set of upheavals form a key part of modern world history.

Beginning with nineteenth-century histories of the French Revolution, and then repeated for all later revolutions, historical approaches to the causes of revolution tended to focus on political factors: the strength or weakening of the state; the wisdom or folly of rulers; the growth of opposition from below. Depending on the writer's view, these factors could also be social and economic. Revolutions were here the outcome of narratives, either of socio-economic change, or of more particular short-term events. In this school, the most influential comparative text was Crane Brinton's *Anatomy of Revolution* (1965) – a work that gave due regard to ideas and leaders but had no theory of cause, and operated very much within the national, bounded, framework of analysis.

A second body of literature on the causes of revolutions emerged out of the sociological and socio-psychological frameworks developed from the 1950s onwards. This focused on why existing, hitherto viable and reasonably stable, social and political systems broke down. Here, explanations varied from the psychological, according to which revolutions were made by 'dissatisfied' persons, groups or classes, to the sociological, stressing dysfunction and disequilibrium in society, to analysis in terms of political sociology, looking at the tensions involved in modernisation and at conflicts over resources within society. Examples include the works of Ted Gurr, Samuel Huntington, Chalmers Johnson and Charles Tilly. They showed a much more elaborated sense of social causes, but also tended to operate with the bounded system characteristic of sociology, and gave little space to the role of ideas or belief.

Finally, in the 1970s, came explanations in terms of broad macro-historical change, influenced particularly by Karl Marx and Max Weber. These downplayed agency, or short-term causes of personality or politics, and looked instead at longer-term social and economic change, and, in particular, at how a combination of factors, external as well as internal, weakened the state. Individuals, parties and ideologies were downplayed and greater emphasis was put on how international factors – wars, changes in the world economy and trade – undermined the power of states. Revolutions ceased to be events that took place within specific countries, as most historical and socio-psychological analysis assumed, and became, rather, part of the broader conflict of states and social groups on the international stage. Here, the central study was Theda Skocpol's *States and Social Revolutions* (1978), which, apart from its striking neglect of political process, ideas and leadership, also tended to reduce international factors to interstate war – an important international cause but far from being the only one.

No consensus was ever reached on these issues, and within each of the three broad camps there were disagreements. There were two good reasons why no such unity could be achieved. One was history itself: no sooner was a theory of revolution formulated, by academics or by revolutionaries, and accepted, than events jumped up to correct it: the vision of revolution as a necessarily violent but still positive pathway to the creation of a modern liberal order, based on the American and French cases of the eighteenth century, was contradicted by the creation of the authoritarian USSR, the touchstone for twentieth-century revolutions; the hegemony of the Bolshevik model of proletarian revolution, dominant after 1917, was rebuffed by the upsurge of revolutions made by a previously disparaged class, the peasants, in China in 1949, and later in parts of Africa and Latin America; the implicitly 'progressive' nature of revolutions for liberals or Marxists, found it hard to cope with the Islamic revolution of Iran, led by clergy who stated their goal as being to restore the seventh-century model of state and society associated with the Prophet Muhammad, while Skocpol's denial of the role of agency, enunciated in her 1978 book, was quickly challenged by the voluntary seizures of power by Khomeini in Iran (February 1979) and the Sandinistas in Nicaragua (July 1979). Finally, the historical perspective of revolutions as state building and historically irreversible seemed to crumble in the face of the mass rejection of Soviet-style communism in Eastern Europe between 1989 and 1991.

Equally important, however, were disputes on methodological issues. Lenin once observed that revolutions could only happen when *two conditions* were met: the ruled could not go on being ruled in the old way, *and* the rulers could not go on ruling in the old way. Most studies of revolution have looked at those wanting change – the rebels and revolutionaries – but also important is why the old state, possessed of the instruments of coercion, should collapse. One factor is the weakness, corruption and indecisiveness of the rulers – a remarkably recurrent theme from Charles I, through Louis XVI, Nicholas II and, more recently, the Shah of Iran. Gorbachev, too, while certainly not corrupt, was for all his display of briskness curiously indecisive and lacking in political perception, perhaps mercifully so. It is also important to consider not only the social and economic context prompting rebels to act but also their will, organisation and mobilisation. Revolutionaries often claim to have made revolutions and, even when their exaggerations are discounted, an element of conscious will, and vision, does seem to be important. In addition, while those wishing to discredit revolutions often invoke alien or foreign forces, they do have a genuine point; wars weaken states, even if they win them, and ideas and examples from abroad, even if inaccurately received, can contribute to political discontent.

To some extent, the revolutions of modern history, especially since 1789, form a separate historical set of upheavals – part of the 'history' of competing world visions that Francis Fukuyama now says, with some justice, has ended. The two centuries between 1789 and 1989 make up a separate era, marked by a particular set of ideological assumptions – about social change, novelty, the path to an imagined modernity – caused by the very same conflicts with modernity that prompted modern wars, and are quite distinct from earlier revolts and rebellions. Whether 1991 marked not only the 'end of history' but also 'the end of revolutions' is still, however, a matter for speculation, and anxiety, although, for some, it does offer an element of hope for the twenty-first century.

Further reading

Crane Brinton: *Anatomy of Revolution* (Vintage, 1965)

Ted Gurr: *Why Men Rebel* (Princeton University Press, 1970)

Fred Halliday: *Revolution and World Politics: The Rise and Fall of the Sixth Great Power* (Macmillan, 1999)

Theda Skocpol: *States and Social Revolutions: A Comparative Analysis of France, Russia and China* (Cambridge University Press, 1978).

Commentary by Chris Bunting
Freelance writer

In the title sequence for the 1970s British sitcom *Citizen Smith*, the hero 'Wolfie' Smith, leader of the Tooting Popular Front and general Marxist revolutionary about town, used to stride out from Tooting Broadway Station whistling an up-tempo version of 'The Red Flag'. The camera followed Wolfie, clad in the obligatory afghan coat and a Che Guevara beret, as he whistled his way up Tooting High Street and kicked a can across the railway bridge. At the other side of the bridge, towering above the street below, he thrust his fist in the air, struck a heroic pose, and bellowed across south London at the top of his voice: 'Power to the People.'

Sadly for Wolfie, there was never a revolutionary mob waiting to surge forward at his rousing words. All he ever got were two lollipop-sucking ten-year-olds in an empty street with no idea of what on earth he was talking about. It took our hero four series, and endless revolutionary schemes, to realise that his dreams of being swept to power and lining his enemies against a wall for 'one last fag, then bop, bop, bop' were just that. Tooting was happy in its chains.

Every age and every place has its Wolfie Smiths. There is always someone hoping (in some societies more privately than in others) that the social and political system will be turned on its head. And, as for Wolfie, realisation of these desires has, more often than not, been a distant fantasy. For every storming of the Bastille, there have been 10,000 Socialist Worker Party meetings in nearly empty halls spent grumbling about the apathy of the masses.

Just occasionally, however, somebody puts their head above the parapet, shouts 'Power to the People' and finds a chorus of excited voices shouting back. And when the idea of revolution catches hold of a society, all hell can break loose. Norms that have governed for generations may, all at once, be consigned to the dustbin of history. The powerful, within a matter of hours, may become hunted prey. What was right may become wrong. At such times, the word 'revolution' signifies more than Che Guevara chic, it is a literal description of the experience of living through funda-mental change.

But why do these radical changes happen in certain places and certain periods and steadfastly refuse to happen, whatever the pleadings of the Wolfies of this world, in others?

Historians and political practitioners have grappled with the question for centuries. The Chinese classic text the *I Ching*, composed about three millennia ago, said of the seizing of power by the founders of the Shang dynasty, T'ang and Wu: 'Heaven and earth undergo their changes and the four seasons complete their revolution. T'ang and Wu led insurrections according to the will of Heaven and in response to the wishes of men. Great indeed is the significance of such a time. Change of any kind is generally viewed by people with suspicion and dislike; therefore it must be instigated gradually. When change is necessary, it will only be approved after it has been seen to work. A proven necessity beforehand, and a firm correctness throughout: these are the conditions under which revolutions can be successfully brought about.'

Within the Western tradition, the ancient Greeks devoted much thought to such violent seizures of political power, but we must be careful about assuming too much similarity between their approach to the problem and our modern view of political change. In fact, the word most often used by the Greeks to refer to unconstitutional change – 'stasis' – means the exact opposite of our word 'revolution'. Rather than describing the rapid movement of a 'revolution', 'stasis' talks about 'rigidity' and a lack of flexibility. So how could such a word refer to violent political change? Confusingly, the Greek concept is focusing on what classical thinkers generally agreed to be the *cause* of revolution – the sclerosis and rigidity of a bankrupt political order – rather than its *effect*, rapid change.

For Aristotle (384–322 BC), who provides a pragmatic guide to 'stasis' in *Politics V*, political disorder is triggered by all kinds of short-term causes (changes in the factional balance of power, for instance) and differs according to the society in which it occurs. But, fundamentally, 'stasis' is about a loss of fluidity in politics and the underlying spirit of cooperation on which a political system relies. When factions become hardened in their positions and resist the smooth interplay of society, then the political order has become sclerotic and revolution is on the cards.

The word '*revoluzione*' does not make its first appearance until the late medieval period in Italy. The root of the word was the verb '*revolvere*', to turn round and to turn back, and its use in this period reflected a common contemporary assumption that history had a cyclical flow. For the Italians, according to Fred Halliday, writing in *Revolution and World Politics* (1999), 'radical change was above all something which returned to a previous era'. What is strikingly absent from both this and the classical view of revolutions is any idea that they are part of some grand 'progress' in history, a concept that was later to mark our thinking on the subject deeply. For ancient Greek thinkers, including Plato, the overthrow of governments through 'stasis' was seen as part of a process of degeneration. Revolutions were symptoms of a breakdown in the health of a political system – like the heart attacks that kill an old, inflexible man.

By contrast, thinkers in the late eighteenth century associated revolution with youth, with historical progress, and with the growing up (rather than ageing) of a polity. One event, the French Revolution, was largely responsible for this change. Alexis de Tocqueville (1805–1859) wrote: 'No previous upheaval, however violent, has aroused such passionate enthusiasm, for the ideal the French Revolution set before itself was not merely a change in the French system but nothing short of a regeneration of the whole human race.'

Georg Wilhelm Friedrich Hegel (1770–1831), who developed the idea that history was not a series of meaningless chances but 'the march of reason in the world', explained the French Revolution as the overthrow of an 'utterly irrational state of things'. He wrote: 'The idea of right asserted its authority all at once, and the old framework of injustice could offer no resistance to its onslaught . . . Not until now had man advanced to the recognition of the principle that thought ought to govern spiritual reality. This was accordingly a glorious mental dawn.'

This idealism was later discarded by Karl Marx (1818–1883) and his followers in favour of a rigorously materialist world view, but its assertion that history is progressive and that revolutions are instruments of that progress is deeply ingrained in the dominant revolutionary tradition of the twentieth century. According to the Marxists, revolution is likely to happen when social and political institutions frustrate economic progress. Modern revolutions are understood as the inevitable triumph of the urban industrial working class, the proletariat, over the trustees of doomed and outdated forms of economic organisation.

The Marxist tradition has produced so many, often contradictary, analyses of the nature of revolutions that it is impossible to encompass them here. Important branches include Leninism, with its emphasis on the role of the revolutionary party, tactics and leaders in playing midwife to a revolution, and Maoism, which stressed the ability of the communities from which a revolution arises to shape its particular form. The overall approach, however, has remained deeply marked by a post-French Revolutionary view of revolution as a tool of historical progress.

Outside the mainstream Marxist tradition, however, revolutionary analysis since the 1950s has been characterised by a slow retreat from the high tide of historical optimism towards a more contingent view of revolutions as expressions of specific problems within particular societies. Much modern analysis sometimes seems to have more in common with Aristotle and the ancient Greeks than Marx and Hegel.

Chalmers Johnson's *Revolutionary Change* (1966), for instance, expounds a sociological analysis of revolution reminiscent of Aristotle's idea that societies rely on shared values to maintain order. According to Johnson, social and political institutions rely on, and are legitimated by, value systems which are internalised by the population through processes of socialisation. When such value systems and the environment become 'dis-synchronised' because of either internal or external disruptions, Johnson says, the population can become disoriented and open to conversion to revolutionary ideologies offering alternative value systems. The existing authorities, unless they act quickly to 'resychronise' themselves to the environment, can find themselves relying on raw power to maintain their control and vulnerable to violent attempts at political change.

Ted Gurr, in *Why Men Rebel* (1970), offers an even more psychologically based theory of revolution. Gurr argues that 'political violence' happens when large numbers of people become angry at gaps between what they feel they are entitled to from a social system and what they actually get. Such anger is not always expressed as revolution – revolutionary action requires a high level of organisation – but, for Gurr, revolution is essentially a function of mass psychology.

Structural theories advanced by thinkers like Theda Skocpol and Ellen Trimberger, on the other hand, have maintained the

Marxist view that revolution is the product of objective economic and social conditions rather than subjective experience. They too, however, have backed away from a simplistic equation of revolution with historical progress. In recent history, they point out, revolutions have occurred in primarily agrarian, relatively backward states challenged by military and economic threats from more advanced nations. Instead of being instruments of modernisation, they have been about resisting foreign incursions. Some revolutions have followed modernising policies as part of such resistance, for example Japan's Meiji Revolution or the Russian Revolution, but others have taken an opposite path, including Cambodia in 1975 or Iran in 1978.

Skocpol even questions whether 'revolution', in the traditional sense of a violent and cataclysmic seizure of power, is even possible any more in advanced industrial nations: 'Even if, especially if, the working classes of the advanced societies should become politically self-conscious revolutionaries on national and international scales – something very different and more difficult to achieve than the local level class organisation that lay behind peasant revolts in France, Russia and China – they would still have to contend with the repressive capacities of existing states . . . It seems highly unlikely that modern states could disintegrate as administrative-coercive organisations without destroying societies at the same time.' Maybe Wolfie was just barking up the wrong tree?

Why do economies collapse

Why do economies collapse?

Harold James
*Professor of history and international affairs at the Woodrow
Wilson School, Princeton*

One of the comfort blankets to which modern people clutch is the idea that there was only ever one big simultaneous world depression, produced by such an odd confluence of causes as to be unique: the legacy of the First World War and of the financial settlement of reparations and war debt; the chaotic banking system of the largest economy of the world, the United States; and inexperience in handling monetary policy in a world that was still pining for metallic money. Since these circumstances were unique, they cannot occur again. Right, Governor, as one might say to the head of a central bank. Historians, however, would be more cautious.

A great deal of historically informed literature on globalisation makes the point that there were several periods before this in which increased worldwide integration came to a halt and was reversed with painful consequences. While the most familiar precedent for modern globalisation is that of the late nineteenth and early twentieth century, ending with the inter-war Great Depression, there were also earlier epochs of integration: the Roman Empire, the economic rebound of the late fifteenth and early sixteenth centuries (the economic backdrop to the Renaissance), or the eighteenth century, in which improved technology and increased ease of communications opened the way to global empires (for Britain and France). All of these previous globalisation episodes ended with wars. Bad policies can wreck individual economies in a whole range of different ways but systemic collapse is a product of militarised conflict. Is this an accident?

There are two major ways in which war undermines globalisation. The first, most obvious, and most studied, way is simply the consequence of the cost of war: the problem of financing unproductive military activity, the disruption of commerce, the suspension of migration and the freezing of capital movements because of security priorities. The second is the tendency for armed conflict, even when its scope is quite small, to provoke international discord in other areas of international interaction. War challenges assumptions about the global distribution of economic and political power.

The idea that war is costly and disrupts 'normal commerce' is well understood in the classic literature of economics. Indeed, for those like Adam Smith who experienced the wars of the American and French revolutions, how could it be otherwise? Smith's first volume of *Wealth of Nations* (1776) closes Book III with the reflection that 'the ordinary revolutions of war and government easily dry up the sources of that wealth which arise from commerce alone'.

Most periods of modern conflict have been accompanied by inflationary war finance, and followed by sharp periods of deflation. The most obvious cause of post-war deflation is the effect of increased government expenditure on interest rates. An alternative way of thinking about this is as the destruction or wearing out of capital in wartime, and consequently higher price of new capital. The rise in real long-term interest rates makes peacetime investment more expensive and depresses activity. This effect is enhanced if governments try to return to pre-war exchange rate systems with prices and wages that have been boosted and distorted by the high levels of wartime demand.

Almost all of the most dramatic historical episodes of sustained deflation came in the aftermath of war. A sustained economic depression followed the

American War of Independence, and accentuated the initial anti-commercial bias of the politics of the new republic. After the Congress of Vienna (1814–15) ended the Napoleonic Wars, Europe experienced decades of deflation, in which industrial investment was costly and the bankruptcy of entrepreneurs frequent. The aftermath of the 1860s civil wars (or wars of unification) in Italy, Germany and the United States all included an immediate speculative bubble, and then the bursting of the bubble (after 1873), with stock-market price collapses, bankruptcies and reduced investment. The First World War was also followed by a brief reconstruction boom in 1919, and then by a collapse in the major Western economies in 1920–1; one decade later came the Great Depression.

Some of these classic effects, in which war produces monetary instability, are still very visible in the aftermath of the major international conflicts of the post-1945 era. The conflicts in Korea and Vietnam both produced inflationary surges, which initially reduced, and then increased, real interest rates, and which corresponded to investment surges and declines. The 1991 Gulf War, however, no longer fits this pattern: both inflation and interest rates fell, although the war was followed by a brief recession, which is generally held by political analysts to have frustrated the re-election of President George Bush in the 1992 election.

One explanation of the changing effects of war in very recent times is that the cost of each war for the major superpower has been falling since the middle of the twentieth century. In today's terms, the Second World War cost about $4,700 billion, Korea $400 billion, Vietnam $572 billion, the 1991 Gulf War $80 billion, and the fighting in the Iraq War of 2003 cost little over $20 billion. It would consequently be appropriate to expect a diminution of the purely fiscal impact of wars, and consequently of their deflationary legacy. Taking a naive approach to the demand for military action and its supply, falling costs should suggest increased demand and a new likelihood of the use of force to effect regime change. The less a war costs, and the fewer the casualties, both military and civilian, the more likely it becomes.

Smith made a similar point about some of the wars of the eighteenth century. The combination of technology, which made war between advanced and backward countries less costly for the advanced country, and new methods of spreading the financial burden of war through the sale of debt instruments, was making war more likely: 'In great empires the people who live in the capital, and in the provinces remote from the scene of action, feel, many of them, scarce any inconveniency from the war; but enjoy, at their ease, the amusement of reading in the news-papers the exploits of their own fleets and armies.'

But wars also lead to questions about the rules that guide economic interaction, both internationally and domestically. All wars, big or small, produce new prob-lems and divisions. Security concerns spill over into eco-nomics. One tradition of thinking about wars (and especially of the smaller scale wars of the late nineteenth-century era of globalisation) suggests that they have eco-nomic origins, and that they are fought – especially in eras of globalisation – because of a wish to control a greater share of global resources. This is familiar to historians and social scientists as the Hobson–Hilferding–Lenin inter-pretation of imperialism. It is largely wrong as an explana-tion of the origins of wars, but very powerful in understanding the political response to them.

The model of the imperialist war that the British liberal John A. Hobson, and the Marxists who adapted his explanation, had in mind was the relatively short, non-total, war that characterised the era of high globali-sation. The Spanish-American war of 1898 that brought the United States into the international system was, unlike the sustained conflicts earlier in the nine-teenth century, a very unequal conflict between the world's fastest growing and largest industrial economy, and a very backward European imperial power. While 274,000 US soldiers were deployed, only 379 were killed. It was soon followed by another unequal conflict, the British conquest of the Boers.

Both of these unequal wars were acutely controversial in domestic politics and could be interpreted as 'land grabs', demands for resources that were scarce: sugar from the Caribbean, and diamonds (from the Kimberley field) and gold in southern Africa. At first the wars produced electorally successful nationalism, with the 1900 British 'khaki election' producing a large Conservative and imperialist vote, and in the United States a surge of popularity for Theodore Roosevelt, who had been the hero of the 1898 war. Then there was a backlash, in which critics pointed out associations between war and the personal gains of a small group of corrupt businessmen and financiers.

In Britain, Leo Chiozza Money, a writer and Liberal MP, denounced the corruption of finance. The Liberals made much of the hypocrisy of the British government for denouncing racial discrimination of the Boers while encouraging massive Chinese immigration to provide labour for the development of southern Africa. They won a stunning electoral victory in 1906. In the United States, the mood turned against the financiers who had bought the election of President William McKinley in 1896. Roosevelt himself began to denounce 'certain malefactors of great wealth' who had appropriated many of the gains produced by public action. Populists presented war and corporate scandal as going hand in hand.

These wars also made international relations significantly more tense. The Boer War was one of the decisive moments in the growing breach between Britain and Germany, with the German Kaiser publicly supporting the Boers. Small conflicts thus set the stage for bigger and more global clashes, in which arguments over the distribution of spoils worsened the international climate.

This capacity of relatively small conflicts to destroy large elements of international agreement looks familiar. And the danger of escalating conflict disrupting globalisation has historical precedents that go back much further than the world of late nineteenth-century globalisation.

The first volume of Edward Gibbon's classic study *The History of the Decline and Fall of the Roman Empire* was (by chance) published in 1776, the year of the signing of the American Declaration of Independence and of Smith's *Wealth of Nations*. Gibbon's advice and Smith's concern about war destroying commerce look immediately relevant today, and quite alarming. Both Smith and Gibbon were thinking, in the wake of the humiliation of a global British commercial and military system, about the problems of what might be termed a reverse of globalisation.

Gibbon begins with praise for the peaceful character of the Emperor Augustus, and of Roman realism and multilateralism: 'Inclined to peace by his temper and situation, it was easy for him to discover that Rome, in her present exalted situation, had much less to hope than to fear from the chance of arms; and that, in the prosecution of remote wars, the undertaking became every day more difficult, the event more doubtful, the possession more precarious, and less beneficial.' This is a fine description of the attractions and perils of economic prosperity. Rome might have basked in consumer prosperity, but this prosperity sucked her into a world of conflict that in turn destroyed her economy.

Further reading

Edward Gibbon: *The History of the Decline and Fall of the Roman Empire* (1776)

Harold James: *The End of Globalization* (Harvard University Press, 2001)

Mancur Olson: *The Rise and Decline of Nations:*

Economic Growth, Stagflation and Social Rigidities (Yale University Press, 1982)

Emma Rothschild: *Economic Sentiments: Adam Smith, Condorcet, and the Enlightenment* (Harvard University Press, 2001)

Adam Smith: *Wealth of Nations* (1776).

Commentary by Simon Targett
Journalist on the Financial Times

'It's the economy, stupid!' This sentence, scribbled on the notice-board in Bill Clinton's campaign office, became the soundbite of the 1992 US presidential election. It described the view that the most important thing in the political process was the health of the economy. So, although George Bush Sr, the incumbent president, had just scored a military victory during the first Gulf War, it was never going to help him win the support of electors suffering unemployment, wage cuts and general economic misery.

There was nothing novel about the comment that the economy was central to the political fortunes of presidents and parties – hence the word 'stupid'. Ever since Aristotle, the Greek philosopher who tutored Alexander the Great and who penned *Politics* in around 335 BC, the economy has been regarded as integral to the body politic.

In modern times, self-styled economists have sought to describe how and why the contemporary economy works. Adam Smith, who published his *Wealth of Nations* in 1776, as American Revolutionaries signed their declaration of independence from the British Crown, was the first great exponent of this. If, however, economists have endeavoured to comprehend the minutiae and the mechanics of the contemporary economy, it is historians – or at least those with a historical perspective – who have answered the much bigger, more panoramic question: why do economies collapse?

The French historian Emmanuel Le Roy Ladurie liked to divide historians into two types: truffle-hunters, who searched for all manner of hidden details, and parachutists, who sought a panoramic view of events. Some truffle-hunters have examined the economic question, focusing on individual countries or particular moments in time: the 'tulipmania' which gripped the Dutch in the 1680s, Ireland's potato famine in the mid 1840s or the Wall Street Crash of 1929. But, for the most part, economic collapse has been a favoured topic of parachutists, who, understanding the reliance of politics on economics, have taken to using words with broader meaning: empire, civilisation, and the like.

The earliest Greek writers described a cyclical process of political development: the rise, the fall, the renewal. It was ancient Rome, however, that provided historians with the best case study for tackling the subject of political – and, implicitly, economic – collapse.

Livy and Tacitus were among the first to tell this story but they were certainly not the last. Sir Walter Raleigh, the Elizabethan adventurer, addressed the subject in his *History of the World* (1614) – one of the first works of historical synthesis – which he wrote in the Tower of London while he was awaiting the executioner's axe. He noted that all the great empires – from Babylon, through Persia, Egypt and Macedon, to Rome – were undone by the hubris and aggrandisement of princes.

In the following century, Edward Gibbon, a historian-cum-politician, published the archetypal study of politico-economic collapse: *The History of the Decline and Fall of the Roman Empire*, which traced the story of the ancient world's greatest power. It did not stop in AD 410, when the Visigoths sacked Rome, the conventional date for the end of empire, but followed the story to 1453, when the Eastern empire in Constantinople finally collapsed before the might of the Ottoman Turks. It was a mammoth work, running to six volumes, a million and a half words, and 8,000 footnotes. British politicians, controlling an even bigger empire, took notes. William Gladstone, Britain's prime minister four times between 1868 and 1894, ranked Gibbon among the three greatest historians of all time.

Yet, for all this, Gibbon offered no pecking order of reasons for the collapse of Rome. For him, unlike the city's rise – 'which may deserve, as a singular prodigy, the reflection of a philosophic mind' – the city's fall was more simply portrayed. 'The decline of Rome was the natural and inevitable result of immoderate greatness,' he wrote. 'Prosperity ripened the principle of decay; the causes of destruction multiplied with the extent of conquer; and as soon as time or accident had removed the artificial supports, the stupendous fabric yielded to the pressure of its own weight.' In drawing this conclusion, he was recalling Livy's observation: *Eo crevit, ut magnitudine laboret sua* (it grew so great that it toppled itself).

Historians have since tried to draw up a list of causes. Michael

Grant, a modern populariser of the classical world, in *The Fall of the Roman Empire: A Reappraisal* (1976), identified a list of thirteen 'defects' or 'disunities' which combined to bring Rome to its knees. But, if Gibbon had no such list, he did offer an alternative way of answering the question of collapse, turning it on its head. 'The story of its ruin is simple and obvious,' he wrote, 'and instead of inquiring why the Roman empire was destroyed, we should rather be surprised that it had subsisted for so long.' This proved an influential way of tackling the problem. Eric Hobsbawm, addressing the fortunes of the British Empire in *Industry and Empire: From 1750 to the Present Day* (1968), talked of 'relative decline' – even though the US and Soviet empires had taken its place as global superpowers. 'The status quo was somewhat shaken, but never utterly interrupted,' he observed. 'We have so far suffered erosion, but not collapse.' In his *History of the World* (1976), John Roberts said that fifth-century writers bewailed the 'collapse' of the Roman Empire so much that 'it is easy to have the impression . . . that the whole society fell apart. This was not so.' In fact, he said, what seized up was the apparatus of the state.

Roberts suggested that this happened because it 'became too big for the demographic, fiscal and economic base which carried it', just as Gibbon had pointed to internal decay as a cause for the collapse. Georg Wilhelm Friedrich Hegel (1770–1831) had made the same point. In *The Philosophy of History*, Hegel presented the first great 'universal history', starting his story in China, and taking the reader through the Greek and Roman worlds, finishing with contemporary Germany. Each civilisation handed over the baton of history to the next, in a one-way path to the present day, as they buckled under the pressure of internal problems. He cited the example of the medieval city, which fostered merchants who would become the standard bearers of the capitalist economic system that would replace the old system of feudalism.

Karl Marx (1818–1883), Hegel's most famous interpreter, went one step further, pointing to the seeds of decay within a capitalist society. In *Das Kapital* (1867), he saw that the capitalist state, where a privileged minority of property owners was predominant, would be replaced by an uprising of the marginalised working class.

In the twentieth century, there was a dramatic rise in the number of people attempting a world or global history and, in doing so, seeking explanations for the collapse of economies, empires or civilisations. At the end of the First World War, H.G. Wells, one of the first great science-fiction writers, started *The Outline of History*, published in 1920, which covered the history of the world from primordial times to the present day. His answer as to 'why the Roman republic failed' was: 'the essence of its failure was that it could not sustain unity'.

As Wells put pen to paper, so too did Oswald Spengler, a German historian, whose *Der Untergang des Abendlandes* (1918–22) traced the 'decline of the West' and contended that each culture was subject to the same laws of growth and decay. Arnold Toynbee, an English classicist, followed Spengler's example. His *Study of History* (1934) divided history into the stories of distinct peoples, each with their own separate past and future. But he did think there were common causes of decline. Like Gibbon, he considered that the 'problem of the breakdowns of civilisations [was] more obvious than the problem of their growths'. He pointed to domestic weaknesses as the primary cause of collapse – not, in other words, the actions of barbarians or foreign powers. 'All the six non-Western civilisations alive today,' he wrote – thinking of Russia, India, China, Japan, the old Ottoman Empire and Arabia – 'had broken down internally before they were broken in upon by the impact of Western civilisation from outside.'

In this period – as in the past – politicians also tried their hand at 'big history', seeking to understand why apparently invincible political systems crumble away. They included Jawaharlal Nehru, who later became India's first prime minister. He wrote *Glimpses of World History* (1934) from his prison cell, just as Sir Walter Raleigh had done more than three hundred years earlier. In a chapter on 'the decline and fall of the Mughal empire in India', he wrote: 'It fell, as almost all empires fall, because of its own inherent weaknesses. It literally went to pieces.'

In the second half of the twentieth century, the pessimism of historians writing during the war years gave way to a new optimism. In 1963, William McNeill argued in *The Rise of the West* that contact with strangers was the major engine of societal change. In describing the decline of the British Empire, McNeill observed that 'if it had been left to its own devices', industrial revolution would have 'died down'. But Britain's industrialism, 'reacting with divergent attitudes and institutions in other lands', acquired a second impetus, and the operators of the old empire, 'like everyone else in the world, had to adjust themselves accordingly'.

Meanwhile, the US had assumed a new primacy, becoming, by 1917, 'a world power', eclipsing Western Europe as the undisputed centre and arbiter of Western civilisation. This has led historians to look for the seeds of the decline and fall of the American Empire. In *The Rise and Fall of the Great Powers: Economic Change and Military Conflict from 1500 to 2000*, written in 1988, Paul Kennedy highlighted a conundrum which has exercised economists, politicians and historians since classical times: to be a great power demands a flourishing economic base, yet by going to war – or, at least, devoting resources to armaments – a great power risks eroding that base, especially in relation to others that devote their resources to productive investment for long-term growth. Given this, he predicted that the hegemony of the US, USSR and other major states would erode, as other nations grew wealthier.

This thesis, which alarmed Washington strategists, has already proved half true. The USSR is now no more, having engaged in a costly cold war with the US. Meanwhile, economists, citing historical precedent, are drawing up scenarios for the day when China eclipses the US. Goldman Sachs, the American investment bank, in a recent report for investors, declared that China would overtake the US as the number-one nation in 2040. The reason for this would be less about American collapse and more about Chinese catch-up. Insofar as there is an answer to the question 'why do economies collapse?', this point about relative decline and the growing burden of an expanding empire would seem to have been the historian's most popular response.

What makes effective laws

What makes effective laws?

Alan Macfarlane

Professor of anthropological science, University of Cambridge

In considering what makes effective laws, it all depends on what we mean by 'effective' – cost-effective? effective in suppressing crime? in providing the security which capitalist economies need? effective in protecting the citizen or subject? These can conflict.

One index of effectiveness is whether there is 'the rule of law', but what does this mean? It could be interpreted as people being prepared to settle disputes through legal process, rather than by force. In most societies, people fear and hate the law, or believe it is weak and corrupt. To persuade people to use law as the normal process of settling disputes is enormously difficult and requires immense political skill and good fortune. It happened early in England, but it is still not widespread in many parts of the world.

It could also be taken to mean that all actions and all power are ultimately under the law. Above the rulers there is something higher; they too are under the law. Most legal systems develop differently. At first the rulers may say: 'We make the laws and we keep the laws.' But after a time they forget the second half of this. They are above the law. So the law does not rule them, they rule the law. You can see this in Stalin's Russia, Chairman Mao's China, or France in the later seventeenth century. There is one law for the powerful and rich and another law for the people.

The 'rule of law' depends on uniform application of laws and a common procedure. It means that the legal process should be separated from the political process, that judges and courts should be independent. All of this is difficult to sustain. Powerful forces – economic and political – are constantly hoping to bias law in their direction.

These separations are particularly fragile in times of war – whether during real wars, such as the Second World War, or during invented or ideological wars, such as the 'wars' against medieval heretics, 'wars' against Satan and his empire of witches, 'wars' against communism in the McCarthy purges of the 1950s, 'wars' against terrorism. In each case, civil liberties are eroded and legal independence crushed. We saw this all too clearly in the United States and Britain as fear and panic were used to justify suspension of normal legal rights following the terrorist attacks on the World Trade Center.

A second index of effectiveness concerns the degree to which people abide by legal decisions. The great problem is to persuade people to accept what is going on in the legal process. The legal process takes people out of their ordinary lives, where they have become entangled in relationships of conflict. It puts them in an arena that is out of normal time and space and rearranges their lives. It takes pressure to persuade people to follow a decision that they may think is against their interest.

To force acceptance, law is often a dramatic and elaborate process. People dress up in strange costumes, the judge sits high up above the court, long words are used in a strangely formal way. There are often dramatic public punishments, as in the so-called 'theatre of Tyburn' where criminals were taken through the streets and executed before the crowds in eighteenth-century England.

A third sense of effectiveness concerns the degree to which the citizens or subjects feel protected by their laws and legal processes. In almost all serious legal cases you have a confrontation between the state and the citizen or subject. The state has almost all the power and the single individual is inherently very weak. So if the state says you are suspected of an offence, how can you defend yourself?

This is why the jury system is so effective. Under this system, where it is the duty of your equals to decide your guilt or innocence, everything is changed. The jury are not themselves on trial but are observers and arbiters. It is one thing to grind down a single individual already accused of an offence. It is entirely different to be able to persuade twelve free individuals, who have agreed on oath, to judge as fairly as possible, without fear or favour.

So the jury acts as a filter to state power, a protection for the single citizen or subject. It is a key institution in any democracy. Most countries in Western Europe had juries of a sort a thousand years ago. The tribes that destroyed the Roman Empire had introduced a legal system of trial by peers in front of travelling judges and this was maintained for over half a millennium.

Yet almost all had given up the jury system by the eighteenth century. One reason was social. Jurist Sir John Fortescue noted in the fifteenth century, when comparing the jury system of England with its absence in France, that juries only work if the countryside is filled with a large class of moderately affluent, educated and independent people who can act as jurymen. England had this class; France did not.

Secondly, most of Europe was recolonised by a form of absolutist Roman law from the fourteenth to the seventeenth century. This was based on an inquisitorial form of justice, where magistrates judged cases without the use of juries. England alone avoided this 'reception' of Roman law and maintained its old jury system. However, there are now increasing calls for its abolition in a wide range of cases, with politicians and other reformers citing the well-known delays, expenses and inefficiencies of allowing people jury trials. That members of the public will gradually find themselves directly confronted by the state, and no longer protected by their peers, will take time to become obvious.

Supplementing the jury is an institution that most of us take for granted but that the great legal historian F.W. Maitland once described as 'a very marvellous institution' and 'so purely English, perhaps the most distinctively English part of all our governmental organization'. These are the magistrates, or what used to be called justices of the peace. Lay magistrates are ordinary, local people, not professionally trained in the law. Some 97 per cent of all cases go no further than the magistrates' court, and even the most serious cases have to be approved by magistrates before they can go on up the legal system.

Magistrates have provided another major protection for the citizen, since they are independent of the government. They are not paid by the state, nor do they answer directly to it. They ensure that justice is local, that it is decentralised, that ordinary citizens (whom they represent) can understand the law. England would have had a very different history without them. This is not only in relation to particular events – for example, they formed the backbone to the resistance to, and ejecting of, James II in the 'Glorious Revolution' of 1688 – but more generally. The very fact of their presence inhibits the pretensions of the executive. Yet, like the jury, they are a threatened species as pressures grow to replace them with stipendiary magistrates – paid and trained lawyers, who inevitably have a closer association with the state.

The degree to which the public trusts the law is deeply affected by its executors, namely the police. Until the middle of the nineteenth century, the English police were local, untrained, ordinary villagers whose duty it was, turn by turn, to act as the constable. They wore no special uniform, carried no special weapons, controlled no police station or local prison. They were literally part of the local community. They were not seen as external, armed, enforcers of the central power in the way that the police were almost everywhere else in Europe.

This localised police force made the laws far more effective. The police knew their community because they were part of it. Because they were generally trusted, information came to them. They did not have to be physically present to deter crime or disorder. Martial policing by an 'occupying power', without local support, is usually disastrous.

The British police force was institutionalised 150 years ago but still retains vestiges of this unique flavour. Officers are still largely unarmed; they are still seen by many ordinary people as reliable, uncorrupt, helpful, perhaps a little pedantic, but basically on their side, although the spread of guns, drugs, racial tensions and violent international crime is currently putting huge pressure on this tradition.

Finally, what makes a law effective is the way in which people feel it runs with their interests and not against them. When it becomes a tool to alter a social structure quickly it can create deep tensions. We can see this in relation to the basic premise of human rights and the law.

It is assumed in modern British law that individuals have rights. Men, women, children, disabled people, even animals and the unborn foetus have intrinsic 'rights'. Very few societies in the world share this view. It is usually thought that an individual only exists as part of a group: he or she has rights in relation to others, and these rights are inseparable from responsibilities; there are no intrinsic rights that come with birth.

The idea that 'life, liberty and the pursuit of happiness' are intrinsic and inextinguishable human rights would be regarded by a large part of the world, even today, and certainly over most of history, as an outrageous claim. When the British imported the idea into India in the nineteenth century it caused immense confusion and upset. A member of a lower caste, a woman, a child, had never been conceived of as having the same intrinsic rights as a high-caste person, a man, a grown-up.

This assumption of individual human rights is a very old feature of English law. It has now spread over the world and become a central doctrine of a new form of mission activity. It has many merits. The protection of the weak (children, women, the poor) against the strong is attractive. The rebalancing of unequal relationships (slaves, wives, factory workers) has benefited from the concept of individual human rights that are protected by the state.

But when taken to extremes, and without sufficient attention to the counterbalancing rights of communities and groups, or the responsibilities that go with the rights, emphasis on human rights can be as dangerous as their absence. It throws the law into disrespect. Social engineering through the law has to be very carefully performed. To many, the obsessive attention to human rights currently being fostered through European legislation is having just this effect.

Legal systems are on a continuum. At one end are those in which the law is a system imposed by the central, absolutist government to keep a reluctant population in sullen submission. We have seen this in many cases from seventeenth-century France to twentieth-century communist and fascist states. At the other extreme, in many simple societies, people run their own legal system through consensus and self-policing.

By chance, and through the advantage of being an island, the English have been able to maintain a position towards the self-enforcing end. This has not only given them a stable and moderately fair and trusted legal system, but has also underpinned their religious and economic freedoms and flexibility. Overblown fears of terrorism, combined with an over-bureaucratic model of government emanating from parts of the European Union project, are in danger of pushing the system rapidly along this continuum towards the absolutist end.

Further reading

John Baker: *An Introduction to English Legal History* (Butterworths, 1979)

John Gray: *False Dawn: The Delusions of Global Capitalism* (Granta, 1998)

Roscoe Pound: *An Introduction to the Philosophy of Law* (Yale, 1954)

Simon Roberts: *Order and Dispute* (Penguin, 1979).

Commentary by Huw Richards
Freelance writer and journalist

All but the most thoroughgoing nihilists – not a group heavily represented among historians – would agree that effective laws are an essential underpinning for any functioning society. Even the radical historian E.P. Thompson (1924–1993), a ferocious polemicist against bad laws, wrote that the rule of law was 'an unqualified human good', while that icon of intellectual conservatives Edmund Burke warned in 1780 that 'bad laws are the worst sort of tyranny'. Yet what makes laws effective – good rather than bad – is something that has been hotly debated over the centuries. To Niccolò Machiavelli, offering advice to state builders in 1517, it may have been 'necessary for him who lays out a state and arranges laws in it, first to presuppose that all men are evil and that they are always going to act accordingly to the nakedness of their spirits whenever they have free scope', but to John Stuart Mill in 1859: 'A state which dwarfs its men, in order that they may be more docile instruments in its hands even for beneficial purposes, will find that with small men no great thing can really be accomplished.'

Allied trades they may be, given the emphasis of most legal systems on precedent, but law and history have tended to make uncomfortable bedfellows. In 1888, F.W. Maitland delivered an inaugural professorial lecture at Cambridge University entitled 'Why the history of English law is not written', arguing, among other things, that one of the difficulties was the mountain of original evidence. He had earlier complained that while Germany continued to produce a flow of printed versions of vital primary sources, British productivity was tailing off. J.H. Baker, giving his inaugural lecture in the same chair 110 years later on 'Why the history of English law has not been finished', also argued that 'history cannot be written in any reliable way until the best evidence has been harvested' and said this was still holding back legal historians.

Yet law was in at the beginning of history as a clearly defined profession in Britain. Arthur Marwick, author of the 1970 historiographical study *The Nature of History*, said that while Oxford University had a Regius professor of history from the early eighteenth century, it was only with the appointment in 1866 of constitutional historian William Stubbs that the basis was laid for the serious study of history at the university.

Medievalist Richard Southern noted in 1961 that constitutional history supplied the intellectual core that history then needed for its survival as a separate intellectual discipline. 'Intellectually it was highly respectable. It was systematic; it gave an organic unity to a large number of otherwise disconnected events. It was difficult.'

Maitland was Stubbs's Cambridge University equivalent. One reason for his enduring appeal is the quality of his writing and historical imagination. He encapsulated the possibilities of legal history in the remark: 'If some fairy gave me the power of seeing the scene of one and the same kind in every age of history of every race, the kind of scene that I would choose would be a trial for murder, because I think that it would give me so many hints as to a multitude of matters of the first importance.' Another reason is the comparative decline of legal and constitutional history in the early part of the twentieth century.

No specialist legal history conference was held in Britain between 1913 and 1972. Introducing papers from the conference that ended that fifty-nine-year drought, Dafydd Jenkins of Aberystwyth University reasoned that: 'Lawyers have always been bemused by the apparent continuity of their heritage into a way of thinking which inhibits historical understanding. "Pure" historians on the other hand have often fled in despair from the mysteries of the law which permeates their history.'

In 1981, John Guy, assistant keeper of public records and later professor of history at St Andrews University, provided an unflattering summation of the field's output: 'With the distinguished exception of the work of F.W. Maitland, legal history has tended to be one of three things; the commemoration of individual lawyers for reasons (usually) of institutional piety; the collection of epitomes of "useful" legal materials, often in alphabetic sequence; and the formula of "epic" and generally "Whiggish" histories in which the whole sequence of English law and legal institutions is chronicled by one man . . . notably from the viewpoint of pure doctrine or the superiority of English to "continental" systems of law and invariably without any semblance of regard for historical, or even legal, materials which were not conventionally available in print.' Maitland, he noted, was at least aware that law had a social context.

Nevertheless, theoretical debates on effective law date at least as far back as the Greeks and Romans. Key running themes include: the extent to which law should have a moral content; whether it should be derived from a unified, coherent code or evolve as common law; and how far it is permissible to dissent from it. Legal theorists have divided broadly into two streams: those who believe in natural law, seeing law as the outcome not of decisions but of underlying principles, something discovered rather than made – an inherently moralistic position – and those who believe in positivism, regarding laws as the outcomes of political decisions, things that reflect the power of those who make them to impose their will, irrespective of morality.

The religious base of classical and medieval societies meant that natural-law theories enjoyed centuries of dominance. It was a credo expressed by the Roman writer and philosopher Cicero (106–43 BC): 'Law is the highest reason, implanted in nature, which commands what ought to be done and forbids the opposite. True law is right reason in agreement with nature. To curtail this law is unholy, to avoid it illicit, to repeal it impossible.' This did not make law wholly inflexible. St Augustine (354–430) offered an early Christian justification for dissent: 'An unjust law is no law at all.' Aristotle had already given natural law one of its most important concepts – equity, defined as 'a correction of law where it is deficient according to its universality'.

Equity was one of the key concepts underpinning the English common-law tradition, which developed by custom, accretion and precedent rather than formal codification of the sort associated with the sixth-century Roman emperor Justinian. Justinian had defined justice as 'the reliable, lasting will to render each his due'. Edward Coke, one of the greatest of English legal thinkers, arguing the case in 1604 for the common-law approach, stated: 'That which hath been refined and perfected by all of the wisest men in the succession of ages, and proved and approved by continual experience to be good and profitable for the common wealth, cannot without hazard and danger be altered or changed.'

Views differed as to how far judges should react to a changing social context. Eighteenth-century Lord Chief Justice Lord Mansfield felt that 'as the usages of society alter, the law must adapt itself to the various situations of mankind', but Sir James Parke, a leading judge in the following century, argued that precedents should be followed 'when they are not plainly unreasonable and inconvenient'. The common-law tradition found one of its most vigorous defenders in William Blackstone, author, in 1765, of *Commentaries* that Baker describes as 'apologising for the status quo with such eloquence'.

Blackstone came under withering assault from Jeremy Bentham (1748–1832), founding father of the positivist school of legal theorists. Bentham devised the 'separation theory', under which law was separated from morality, and argued that 'natural rights is simple nonsense'. He called for laws based on 'the greatest happiness of the greatest number'. His preoccupation with individual liberty – 'every law is contrary to liberty' – continued with Mill, who contended: 'The sole end for which mankind is warranted, individually or collectively, in interfering with the liberty of action of any of their number, is self-protection. The only purpose for which power can rightfully be exercised over any member of a civilised community, against his will, is to prevent harm to others. His own good, either physical or moral, is not a sufficient warrant.' The 'no-harm principle' in turn came under fire from English judge Sir James Stephen (1829–1894), who saw in it a recipe for social disintegration.

This debate was to be reprised a century later, when a 1957 British government study, chaired by Sir John Wolfenden, recommended decriminalising homosexuality on the grounds that it was not the law's function to 'intervene in the private lives of citizens, or to seek to enforce any particular pattern of behaviour'. This drew a counter-polemic from Lord Devlin in his 1965 book *The Enforcement of Morals*, which called for the 'morality of common sense'. Meanwhile, natural law was given fresh impetus by the work of Harvard professor Lon Fuller (1902–1978), who argued that compliance could only be obtained by consistency with broad social values.

One test of legal effectiveness under which legislation over private behaviour is increasingly questioned is that of enforceability. Jean-Jacques Rousseau (1712–1778) argued: 'As soon as it is possible to disobey with impunity, disobedience is legitimate.' It was the scientist Albert Einstein, who remarked in 1935 of the US's experiment of prohibition: 'Nothing is more destructive of respect for the government and the law of the land than passing laws which cannot be enforced,' while US Vice-President Hubert Humphrey proclaimed in 1965 that 'there are not enough jails, not enough policemen, not enough courts to enforce a law not supported by the people'.

Questions of compliance and acceptability have been central for twentieth-century legal theorists. Among the positivists, H.L.A. Hart (1907–1992), whose 1961 *Concept of Law* is among the most influential texts of modern legal theory, saw the effectiveness of law rooted in a set of social rules rather than in patterns of obedience. He rejected morality-based law as likely to lead to threats to liberty, arguing that law worked if enough people conformed to it to persuade others that there was a good reason to behave in this way.

Recent years have seen increased interest in legal and constitutional history in Britain, responding to the significant constitutional changes associated with membership of the European Union from 1973, the devolution of powers to the Scottish Parliament and Welsh Assembly from 1999 and the belief, not wholly confined to the political left, that Margaret Thatcher's governments (1979–90) had exposed serious weaknesses in the existing constitution. David Marquand, in *The Unprincipled Society* (1988), felt that Britain's legal and constitutional inheritance was an obstacle to political reform, while Andrew Adonis and David Butler argued in 1994 that the introduction of the unpopular poll tax reflected the absence of checks and balances on an overpowerful executive. However, John Gray, professor of European thought at the London School of Economics, expressed concern that legal and constitutional formulae might become so ascendant over politics 'that it no longer matters what are the outcomes of political deliberation'. Even so, *The British Constitution in the Twentieth Century* (2003), a multi-authored volume edited by Oxford professor of government Vernon Bogdanor (see this book's chapter on what makes good government), could still credibly be advertised as the first scholarly survey of its subject.

What causes nationalism

What causes nationalism?

David A. Bell
Andrew W. Mellon Professor in the Humanities, Johns Hopkins University

Nationalism is one of those curious phenomena which get blurrier and more confused the closer one looks at them. The word is in common usage, and most educated readers would probably accept without undue quibbling the principal definition provided by the *Oxford English Dictionary*: 'Advocacy of or support for the interests of one's own nation.' Yet scholars of the subject cannot agree if nationalism is a simple sentiment or a political programme, a purely modern occurrence or an ancient one, the product of particular social conditions or a free-floating doctrine. How, then, to proceed?

Following two notable scholars of the subject, Ernest Gellner and Eric Hobsbawm, I have found a fairly narrow definition most useful. Simple feelings of support for, loyalty to or belief in a nation are adequately covered by the terms 'national sentiment' and 'patriotism'. What distinguishes national*ism* is that it refers not simply to feelings, but to organised political doctrines and movements. Furthermore, these doctrines and movements have a clear goal: the construction and/or completion of a particular nation. Nationalist movements, after all, nearly always claim that their nation remains an unfinished project, and suffers from problems that need to be rectified through political action (why else have a movement in the first place?). In some cases, they allege that their nation has been deprived of territories which rightly belong to it; in others, that the national community is diluted or polluted by the presence of national minorities; in others still, that the citizenry has an imperfect knowledge of, and commitment to, national values and traditions, and the national culture. Serbian nationalism of the 1990s, to take one recent example, incorporated nearly all of these grievances. Most often, the ultimate aim of a nationalist programme can be summed up as follows: to unite all members of a nation within its historical territory, where they can collectively exercise political sovereignty, while identifying with the national culture.

Because nationalists justify their actions by invoking the rights of their nation, but simultaneously confess that this nation does not yet truly exist, there is something more than a little paradoxical about nationalism. The paradox is most often resolved through an appeal to history: while the nation may not fully exist today, nationalists explain, it did so once, and still retains all of its rights from that time – indeed, these rights constitute a sacred inheritance. Nationalists, in short, forever situate themselves in a beleaguered and imperfect present, en route between a more glorious past and a more glorious future.

As defined in these terms, nationalism is very much a modern phenomenon, dating from no earlier than the eighteenth century, and originating in Europe. Before this period, European observers did frequently use the word 'nation', which they most often defined as a group of people united by language, law and/or historical tradition, but they saw nations as essentially organic entities – as facts of nature. Nations could be born, grow, wither and die, but they could not be created (or recreated) through systematic political action. The idea that millions of people could be moulded and shaped through politics – given new or improved national loyalties, a new or improved national culture, perhaps even a new or improved national language – was as yet unthinkable. Only with the age of democratic revolutions did the idea begin to gain adherents.

To understand how nationalism first came into being, it is worth paying particular attention to the case of revolutionary France. At the end of the eighteenth century, France was a multi-ethnic, multilingual country in which only a minority of the population spoke standard French. France's kings had never seen this diversity as a pressing political problem, but the revolutionaries of 1789 believed that they could not create a cohesive, democratic community without taking the component peoples of France, and, in the words of the revolutionary Henri Grégoire, 'melting them into the national mass'. They therefore devised ambitious educational programmes to eradicate regional differences, especially in matters of language, and to create a cohesive, unified national community. They imagined legions of instructors bringing the gospel of the nation to the ignorant, *patois*-speaking peasantry, in conscious imitation of the Counter-Reformation missionaries who had earlier gone into the countryside for the very different purpose of ensuring conformity with Catholic teachings. The revolutionaries' policies have continued to inspire French nationalist projects to the present day.

French nationalism, however, was not born solely out of the realm of political thought. When devising their projects, early French nationalists could already take for granted the existence of a cohesive national territory, administered by a centralised state apparatus. They could take for granted the existence of a social and cultural elite that, wherever they lived in France, already spoke standard French, and looked to Paris for cultural guidance. The availability of a reliable postal service and reliable transportation (a network of regularly scheduled long-range carriages), and a burgeoning number of national periodicals, facilitated communication among this elite and allowed them, already in 1789, to imagine themselves as all belonging to the same community. Without these material preconditions, the nationalist project of the revolution would have been difficult to imagine in the first place, let alone to begin implementing.

Perhaps the most important point to retain about French Revolutionary nationalism is that it worked. The prospect of coming together to construct a new, greater national community offered material advantages to potential members of this community, and also a sense of spiritual purpose to people increasingly alienated from traditional Christian teachings (it is no accident that the material paraphernalia of nationalism – parades, processions, flags, anthems, etc. – so closely copies Christian examples, even while turning them to new uses). The French Revolutionaries did not manage to teach all French citizens to speak French (a goal which would only be achieved in the twentieth century), but in other realms they had remarkable success. Most importantly, within a few years after 1789, they forged a truly national, conscript army that quickly overran the frontiers of the *ancien régime* and embarked on a programme of conquest. By the time of Napoleon Bonaparte, French leaders had acquired the ambition not simply to construct a new French nation, but a new 'great nation' that would dominate Europe.

In the two centuries since the revolutionary era, nationalism has manifestly changed the world – and in doing so, it has changed its own causes. Not every nationalist movement has followed the path of the French Revolutionaries. The reason is that the visible success and spread of nationalism have created ever more incentives for people to *become* nationalist, and ever more examples for them to imitate. Even in the early nineteenth century, thinkers outside of France – with the example of the French Revolution before their eyes – found it easier than the French had done to imagine coming together into national communities. In Napoleonic Germany, despite a high degree of political and administrative fragmentation, leading intellectuals came to believe that only the political construction of a united German nation would save them from absorption into France. They therefore spurred resistance to Napoleon, and inspired projects that would come to fruition in the time of Otto von Bismarck. These same intellectuals also began to popularise the idea of a world naturally divided into distinct nations, each with its own particular 'genius', language and culture.

The ultimate success of the Germans in resisting Napoleon – and of other nations as well – in turn inspired further nationalist movements across the Continent in the early nineteenth century, from Greece through the Balkans to multinational Austria–Hungary, to the vast territories of the Tsar. The period around the European revolutions of 1848 is justly called the 'springtime of nations'. By the end of the First World War, these movements had destroyed most of Europe's old empires (only the Russian one managed to preserve itself, as the Soviet Union, for another seventy years), while the Versailles Conference confirmed the principle of 'national self-determination' as the basis for a new world order of states.

As a result of these changes, it is fair to say that throughout the twentieth century, nationalism was less a choice than a necessity for people around the world seeking political power and influence. It had been one thing to embrace nationalism in the early modern world of large, multi-ethnic, religiously inspired empires, where the modern concept of 'nation states' would still have struck most observers as bizarre. It was another thing to embrace it in a world where humankind was assumed to be naturally divided into nation states, and where any political unit which did not conform to this norm would have a hard time fitting into an ever more tightly linked international system. The very word 'international' betrays this preconception, as do the names 'League of Nations' and 'United Nations'.

In the post-First World War world, therefore, nationalism not only remained ubiquitous in Europe itself, but also quickly spread beyond the European Continent. And to their shock, the European imperialist powers discovered that the more cultural influence they wielded – the more they managed to impart their beliefs and values to their colonial subjects – the more they spurred nationalist resistance to their own rule. Thus, in the end, their own colonial empires proved no more successful than Austria–Hungary in staving off nationalism's centripetal demons. In the years after the Second World War they shared its fate, dissolving into often violent and unstable constellations of independent nation states. Forty years later, the Soviet Empire, its own internationalist ideology exhausted, followed as well. As in the Balkans, the examples have often been troubling. But with every population that has shaped itself into a nation state, the pressure has only risen on adjacent populations to do the same. Most of the new nation states have not possessed anything like the material preconditions of nationhood that the French had been able to count on in the eighteenth century. In some cases, they have had no basis other than lines on a colonial map. But the causes of nationalism are no longer what they were in the eighteenth century, for nationalism has become a fundamental principle of the world order. Until this state of affairs changes (and some think the change has already begun), nationalism is something that will remain impossible to avoid.

Further reading

Benedict Anderson: *Imagined Communities: Reflections on the Origin and Spread of Nationalism* (Verso 1983; revised edition, 1991)

David A. Bell: *The Cult of the Nation in France: Inventing Nationalism, 1680–1800* (Harvard University Press, 2001)

Ernest Gellner: *Nations and Nationalism* (Blackwell, 1983)

Anthony D. Smith: *The Ethnic Origins of Nations* (Blackwell, 1986).

Big Questions in History

Commentary by Karen Gold
Freelance writer

'More than 1,000 years before the arrival of Slavs, in the 6th century AD, the lands east of the Adriatic were the home of peoples known to the ancient world as Illyrians, the precursors of the present Albanians.' So runs the history of Kosovo on the web pages of the Albanian Liberation Peace Movement. The Serbian Ministry of Information's website tells a rather different story: 'The Serbs have been living in the territory of Kosovo and Metohija since the sixth century. That territory was the centre of Serbian statehood, an inalienable national treasury, indispensable for the identity of the Serbian people.'

Nationalist feeling comes as naturally to us as breathing, according to the German philosopher Gottfried von Herder. Writing at the end of the eighteenth century, full of Romantic sentiment and Liberal politics, he coined the terms '*Nationalismus*' and '*Volk*' and put forward the argument that nationalism was an organic entity within individual nations, embodied in their language and culture, and existing, consciously or unconsciously, whether anyone wanted it to or not: 'We can assimilate or adopt what is similar to our nature and remain cold, blind and even contemptuous and hostile to anything which is alien and distant . . . A nationality is as much a plant of nature as a family, only with more branches.' We have Herder to thank for the Brothers Grimm, whom he inspired to collect German fairy tales and folklore, the cultural expression of the *Volk*. And we also have Herder to thank for this 'organic' idea of nationalism, which continued virtually unquestioned for more than a hundred years.

It was only really in the twentieth century that historians began to suggest that a belief in nationalism as a natural state of being was useful to political leaders and/or elites who wanted to persuade people to act in a unified way. Such historically pragmatic accounts of nationalism were produced in 1907 by Austrian Social Democrat politician Otto Bauer in *The Question of Nationalities and Social Democracy* and in 1944 by Hans Kohn, who argued in *The Idea of Nationalism* that nationalism was a relatively modern and artificially created state of mind. Historians have focused on key periods and episodes to argue this case, pointing, in particular, to the French Revolution, whose leaders purveyed notions of *la patrie* and a standardised French language in the hope of uniting an untidy scattering of peasants, speaking different dialects, across the newly liberated land. They have traced the way the nineteenth-century Napoleonic and British empires – both more administratively intrusive than their imperial predecessors – aroused resentment while, in Europe at least, failing to fill the faith gap vacated by religion and divinely appointed rulers. Resistance leaders in an unbroken line from Italy's Guiseppe Mazzini, through Ireland's Daniel O'Connell, to India's Mahatma Gandhi, this argument goes, all saw nationalism as a way of uniting and inspiring the disaffected masses to reject their oppressors in the name of creating, or recreating, a nation.

Some historians, like Elie Kedourie of the London School of Economics (the LSE has been rich soil for nationalism theories to flourish), have argued that the main reason why nationalism spread in these circumstances was because it was an ideology that appeared in the right place at the right time. Alienated peoples were shown it, and they bought it. Marxist and proto-Marxist thinkers, in particular Eric Hobsbawm and Ernest Gellner, pre-eminent nationalism theorists for the past twenty years, were more sceptical. (Marx himself virtually ignored nationalism as a horizontal distraction from vertical class conflict.) The anthropologist Gellner, in *Encounters with Nationalism* (1994), argued that nationalism arose out of pressures created by the Industrial Revolution, when people from different backgrounds, speaking different dialects, converged on the city and had to be welded into a literate and retainable workforce. So the state created a common language, a common past and a common culture for them. Benedict Anderson, in *Imagined Communities: Reflections on the Origins and Spread of Nationalism* (1991), said the state relied particularly upon 'print capitalism' to achieve this. Nationalism arose thanks to industrial society, he said. But without propaganda it would not have survived and flourished.

This view of nationalism as originating from above was criticised by Hobsbawm as inadequate, even though true. The artefact of nationalism cannot be understood without understanding the assumptions, hopes, needs, longings and interests of ordinary people under capitalism, he argued, in particular in *Nations and Nationalism since 1780* (1990). The myths and histories which nations created, about themselves but also about each other, only spread because the working class needed to believe in them.

Why did they need to? Answers to that question take us into an entirely different realm of explanations (though glancing back to Herder). Sociobiologists have argued for a genetic predisposition to nationalism: members of a group who believe they have a claim to their own territory are likely to defend it more successfully than those who doubt it, or even hold high-minded principles about sharing it with others. Cultural primordialists, such as the American anthropologist Clifford Geertz, hold a similar position, arguing that territory and kinship are inescapable cultural givens. Psychologists like Harold Isaacs in *Idols of the Tribe* (1975) and Joshua Searle-White in *The Psychology of Nationalism* (2001) have also put forward related theories, positing a universal tendency for people to consider other groups less important than their own, and to form stereotypes about them. Horror stories which circulate about other nations – from competing cruelties in Kosovo, to unsubstantiated rumours of mass rapes and killings attributed by both sides in the First World War, to the ancient blood libel believed of the Jews – seem to substantiate this argument.

But historians have criticised it as problematic. Anthony Smith, professor of nationalism and ethnicity at the LSE, says: 'The trouble is that psychologists tend to equate nations with groups. But there are many groups in the world, and they are not all necessarily nations . . . And there are some nations where everyone doesn't even speak the same language, like Switzerland. Ideas about groups really don't get to the specificity of nationalism.'

Much of the debate about nationalism's longevity, and therefore, by implication, what causes it, depends on definitions. Should it be defined as a specific political programme or a more cultural movement? Smith believes that nationalism's roots are in culture. That makes him a 'perennialist' – someone who believes that nationalism precedes the eighteenth century, though in less sophisticated forms. He suggests that foreshadowing the modern nation are 'ethno-symbols', constructed on language and a vernacular literature, but also on less obvious elements: memory, value, myth, symbolism, landscape. The idea of nationalism may be modern, but its roots are in a distant shared past, he argues.

Another perennialist, the late Leeds University theologian Adrian Hastings, pointed to fourteenth- and seventeenth-century England as periods when national identity was particularly strong; others argue that the Jews and Armenians sustained powerful national identities over millennia. Mazzini, formulating nineteenth-century Italian nationalism against Napoleonic France, passionately defended the cultural roots of his movement: 'They [Italians] speak the same language, they bear about them the impress of consanguinity, they kneel beside the same tombs, they glory in the same tradition, they demand . . . to contribute their stone to the great pyramid of history.'

Ironically, there was virtually no public or academic interest in the roots of nationalism before and after its florid expression in two world wars. Instead, peak times for academic exploration of nationalism's causes have been the 1960s, prompted by African and Asian independence, and the late 1980s and early 1990s, following the break-up of the Soviet Union and Yugoslavia. The argument here has been whether nationalism is the cause or the product of the break-up of old states and the creation of new ones. American sociologist Rogers Brubaker, for example, has argued that the organisation of the Soviet Union into component parts was what taught people to think of themselves as Lithuanian or Ukrainian. In contrast, Michael Hechter, in *Containing Nationalism* (2000), and Czech political theorist Miroslav Hroch point to social and linguistic ties and to a memory of a common past as the trigger for claiming nationhood – though still prompted by historical circumstance rather than any organic drive.

Recently sociologists, particularly on the left, have debated to what extent a 'new nationalism' is appearing in Europe, expressed as anti-immigrant feeling, and how far it is driven by identity or by class interests. The fundamental issue between them is the same as that between Kedourie, Gellner and Hobsbawm: to what extent is this nationalism attributable to a shared ideology, to frustration among individuals who seek an identity having been disappointed by what the twentieth-century state offers them, or to pressures from above to stand together and conform?

Whatever the case, this is nationalism within identified

nations. Nationalism among people who are not yet nations has another very modern cause, historians argue, which is that today's world structures will only hear the voices of people through the representation of a nation state. 'Once almost the whole world is organised into nation states then if you want to be recognised as a legitimate entity you have to be a nation state,' says David Bell. 'So it is almost inevitable that nationalism will follow.'

It is almost inevitable but not entirely. The urge to create, or recreate nations in the dismantled Soviet Union was not uniformly strong, he says. The Russian Federation remains a federation. In central Asia, religious forces seem to be exerting a more powerful pull than nationalist ones.

So are we about to see a decline in nationalism across the world, to be replaced by globalisation or religion? The way people see the future of nationalism depends very much on the explanations they credit for its past, says Smith. 'If you think nationalism is a given in history, then you will think it is going to be around for a long time. If you think it is a completely modern phenomenon, then you might or might not think it is going to pass more or less quickly away.'

Why do wars begin

Why do wars begin?

Thomas Palaima

*Professor of classics at the University of Texas, Austin, where he
teaches war and violence studies*

? Why do wars begin? The simple answer is they
never end. Peace is an illusion conjured up by a
version of the old Roman magic trick: 'Where
they make a desolation, they call it peace.' The full
implications of Tacitus's oft-quoted observation can be
translated like this: 'Use your advanced military technology and overwhelming superiority in human and
natural resources to create a wasteland. Call it peace.
The people back home will believe you. They want to
believe in their own benignity.'

Do you doubt this? Then notice that peace always
comes with qualifiers. Take A. J. P. Taylor's explanation
of the widespread romantic innocence that the 'war to
end all wars' shattered: '(T)here had been no war
between the Great Powers since 1871. No man in the
prime of life knew what war was like.' In August 1914,
the nearly 22,000 British soldiers who died in South
Africa between 1899 and 1902 were not around to tell
stories. Those among the 425,000 Boer War veterans
who were still alive were past their prime. And South
Africa was not a great power – nor were the Zulus,
Ashanti, Afghanis or other peoples butchered in colonial wars throughout this period of European peace.

War is endless. As Paul Fussell remarks in *The
Great War and Modern Memory* (1975): 'The idea of endless war as an inevitable condition of modern life
would seem to have become seriously available to the
imagination around 1916.' He catalogues the wars that
have made the imagined real: the Spanish civil war, the
Second World War, the Greek civil war, the Korean War,

the Arab-Israeli war and the Vietnam War. Orwell published the canonical modern myth of eternal war in 1948. Events have proved him prescient and timeless. Ancient Greek history had already proved him right.

Among recent students of war, Philip Bobbitt, in *The Shield of Achilles: War, Peace and the Course of History* (2002), comes closest to seeing war for what it is. He thinks and writes from the perspective of modern nation states and international diplomacy, but his title alludes to Homer's *Iliad*, and he begins by considering Thucydides' reassessment of the stops and starts in what the Athenian general-in-exile eventually identified as a continuous war that ravaged the entire known world. We now call it the Peloponnesian War and place it at 431–404 BC, thereby creating the comforting illusion that the founders of our Western cultural tradition unwisely let war out of its cage for a nearly disastrously long time, but eventually forced it back inside. However, endless war was an inevitable condition of ancient Greek life.

Thucydides, like other Greeks, distinguished between periods of formally declared war and periods of official peace. But he also knew the primary texts of Hesiod and Homer and enough about contemporary diplomatic and strategic affairs, and human nature, to grasp that *eris*, 'strife, contention, political discord', was a constant force within and among the ancient Greek *poleis*, or city states, and that competing elements within most *poleis* or the controlling powers within individual *poleis* would find, with terrible regularity, true causes (*aitiai*) or pretexts (*prophaseis*) for open civil or interstate warfare. Thucydides took for granted that they would do so single-mindedly in their own interests.

Bobbitt similarly argues that the major armed conflicts of the twentieth century make up a single epochal war, the 'long war of the nation state' and that between 1914 and 1990, 'despite often lengthy periods in which there [was] no armed conflict, the various engagements of the war never decisively settle[d] the issues that manage[d] to reassert themselves through conflict'. If they were alive today, Thucydides and Herodotus would agree with Bobbitt that the periods of so-called peace were intervals when the competing nation states were inevitably preparing for the next phase of open war, even if citizens and leaders of these nation states believed peace had really come.

For the 'long war' view, read Herodotus' prose *Iliad* about the fifth-century war that defined his times. Herodotus wrote about the millennium-long aggressive dance between Greeks and non-Greeks that culminated in the two Persian wars between 490 and 479 BC. Everything in his sprawling nine-book amalgamation of geography, ethnography, anthropology, journalism, history and field recordings of folk tradition relates to the growth of power, the intricate thread of causation and the fundamental differences in defining cultural attitudes that brought allied Greek and Persian forces into confrontation at Marathon, Thermopylae, Salamis and Plataea.

Herodotus would recognise the continuation of his long war between East and West in the current conflicts and tensions involving Israelis and Palestinians, the US and terrorist organisations such as al-Qaeda, the Greeks and Turks on Cyprus, and the wars in Afghanistan and Iraq. *New York Times* journalist Thomas Friedman was being Herodotean in *From Beirut to Jerusalem* (1995) when he observed that Arabs, Jews and Christians in Lebanon and Israel were 'caught in a struggle between the new ideas, the new relationships, the new nations they were trying to build for the future, and the ancient memories, the ancient passions and ancient feuds that kept dragging them back into the past'. And the past means war.

Thucydides tracks how a new strain of war virus, Athenian imperial aggression, develops and spreads in a 'long war' between superpower-dominated city-state coalitions that, like Bobbitt's twentieth-century war, lasts nearly eighty years. Thucydides' 'long war' begins with a fifty-year cold war between an established super-power necessarily conservative in foreign policy (Sparta) and an emerging superpower addicted to its own superabundant interventionist energies (Athens). The Athenian virus eventually drives Athens and Sparta and their allies into a twenty-seven-year world war.

Thucydides' *History of the Peloponnesian War* does not so much analyse why war begins as study how and why war, as an assumed near-constant, reaches new levels of violence, what forms it takes and why human beings aid war.

The best way to see what Thucydides has to say about why wars start is to read Paul Woodruff's anno-tated 1993 translation with commentary, *On Justice, Power and Human Nature: The Essence of Thucydides' History of the Peloponnesian War.* By far the most impor-tant of these subjects is 'power'.

Thucydides compresses Herodotus' nine books into a twenty-five-paragraph analysis of the growth of power in Greek prehistory and history. He demon-strates that human communities are organised for Dar-winian competitive purposes, to acquire and then exploit and defend the limited natural resources avail-able to them. The more successful will convert the energies they have mobilised to ensure their survival into aggressive acquisition of resources, and subjuga-tion of rival communities, to improve the security and material well-being of their own citizens. Dominant states will develop high cultures and use high-minded concepts and ideals to disguise their aggressions.

Like fifth-century BC Athenians, modern Euro-peans and Americans can afford to be concerned about abstract concepts such as justice. Because of our successful use of force in the past and present, we control and consume an imperial share of the world's resources and believe in the illusion of peace. Thucy-dides concentrates on resources, power and state self-sufficiency (*autarkeia*). He juxtaposes his analyses of Pericles' funeral oration, the plague in Athens and Pericles' last speech to tell us all we need to know about imperial self-conceptions promulgated as self-justifying political spin, the fragile nature of codes of civilised human behaviour, and the need for unflinching use of military power to gain and secure empire.

If war is a stern teacher, the Greeks were very sternly taught. Lincoln MacVeagh, US ambassador to Greece, observed in a letter to President Franklin Roosevelt on Christmas Day 1940, 'The history of Greece is at least 50 per cent discord.' A.G. Woodhead, author of the standard guide to Greek historical inscriptions, quotes MacVeagh to correct him: 'Ninety-five per cent, on the record as we have it, would be nearer the mark.' War was reality in ancient Greece. I doubt whether many families during any of the four generations of fifth-century Athens were without the experience of a father, husband, brother, son or close male relative risking or losing his life in battle. The city itself was under virtual siege conditions for much of the final three decades of its one truly great century. In a single six-year operation in Egypt mid-century, the Athenians lost an estimated 8,000 men, roughly 18 to 25 per cent of their adult male population. And, according to conservative estimates, the Athenians would have had their own 'lost generation' during the Peloponnesian War, in which at least 30,000 adult male citizens died.

The Greeks would have had no illusions about war and peace of the sort that prompted Freud at the outset of the First World War to write his essay 'Thoughts for the Times on War and Death: I. The Disillusionment of the War'. Freud attributes the trauma caused by the Great War to the enormous chasm between the artificial morality of modern civilised society and human behaviour in times of war. No such chasm existed in the fifth century BC. Young men learned about war from the *Iliad*. Homer's epic showed them the true costs of war and it portrayed the many contradictions in human behaviour within an army on active campaign and within a city state under siege.

No Greek would ever have forgotten that his community was constantly under threat from rival communities. The plays of Aristophanes convey an appreciation of the benefits for common citizens of a cessation of armed conflict. But an Athenian farmer would never have mistaken the absence of active campaigning for what we call peace, and he would be perplexed that we have to ask why wars begin.

Further reading

Philip Bobbitt: *The Shield of Achilles: War, Peace and the Course of History* (Alfred A. Knopf, 2002)

S. Freud: 'Thoughts for the Times on War and Death: I. The Disillusionment of the War', in E. Jones (ed.), *Sigmund Freud: Collected Papers* (Basic Books, 1959), vol. 4, pp. 288–304.

Paul Fussell: *The Great War and Modern Memory* (Oxford University Press, 1975)

J. Rich and G. Shipley (eds): *War and Society in the Greek World* (Routledge, 1993)

R.B. Strassler (ed.), *The Landmark Thucydides* (Simon & Schuster, 1996)

L. Tritle: *From Melos to My Lai: War and Survival* (Routledge, 2000)

P. Woodruff (ed. and trans.): *On Justice, Power and Human Nature: The Essence of Thucydides' History of the Peleponnesian War* (Hackett, 1993).

New Zealander David Low summed it up perfectly. In a cartoon for
the *Evening Standard* in May 1943, he depicted a herd of sheep gath-
ered outside an imposing government building to hear the croco-
diles, snakes and vultures on the podium announce: 'My friends, we
have failed. We just couldn't control your warlike passions.' Here,
ironically counterpointed, are two of the traditional explanations for
the outbreak of war: popular (sometimes nationalist) passion and
elite calculation, the former tragically compounded by gullibility
and the latter brutally by cynicism.

The word 'war' claims a certain dignity to its operations and
obviously means more than 'absence of peace', but it is not easy to
define. Only a small proportion of history's large-scale outbreaks of
violence began with some kind of formal declaration or even at an
identifiable moment. Exactly when a raid, a vendetta, a rebellion – or a
police operation – becomes a war often depends on who is doing the
defining, and why. Some, like historian John Keegan, see the 'Western
way of warfare', with two clearly defined armies locked together in a
killing spree, as normative, but there are many other forms.

Some wars are exercises in grabbing loot or land, pure and
simple – and many cultures have made no apologies about this: the
Germanic tribes that took over the Roman Empire, and the Mongol
hordes that built up the largest land empire the world has ever
known, sought no further justification for their actions. But others –
and this is particularly true in the case of wars fought by settled civilisations with developed moral codes – in a tradition dating back at
least to the writings of St Augustine in late antiquity, felt it imperative to define a 'just war' and assert the justice of the cause of the
day before urging others to die for it.

Just as it takes two to argue, so it takes two to make a war.
Hitler's invasion of Czechoslovakia in 1938 – however immoral –
did not involve war, whereas the invasion of Poland the next year did
because it was actively resisted, first by the Poles and then by their
allies, France and Britain. The fact that both sides have to opt to
fight explains why so often both sides can claim they are fighting
defensively.

There has long been a pessimistic argument that conflict between humans is a natural condition. A variation of this is the Marxist belief in the inevitability of conflict between classes, and between the states that represent class interests. Such arguments pass the question of the origin of war back to the philosophers, theologians, anthropologists, psychologists and biologists. But it is historians who can account for particular outbreaks at particular times. For if these disciplines tell us it is somehow inevitable for humans to show a propensity for war, then they throw up further questions: why is warfare not permanent and universal? why and how do wars end? why and how do people strive to prevent them or organise affairs so that they can be avoided altogether?

One explanation is that if, as nineteenth-century military strategist Carl von Clausewitz proposed, warfare is an extension of politics by other means, then logically politics is also a substitute for warfare, and so the profession of diplomacy aims to manage conflict without resort to violence. Diplomats have a stake in maintaining the status quo, or allowing change in small, manageable steps, whereas warriors look for cataclysmic and sudden change. Wars occur when diplomacy fails to allow for the necessary steps to occur smoothly or quickly enough – and the reasons can be varied. A.J.P.Taylor, in his work on the origins of war in the twentieth century, argued – to the dismay of many – that it might occur without any party having responsibility for the breakdown in order.

Not all breakdowns in international relations occur as a result of the decisions of the elite: some conflicts are simply too visceral to be managed rationally through diplomatic channels, perhaps the results of ideological, religious, nationalist or racist hatreds arising from popular feeling. Here, there may indeed be a popular clamour for war, though it may be manipulated by those who stand to gain from the conflict. The balance between popular demand and internal politics is often debated: Fritz Fischer's study of the origins of the First World War, for example, saw the bellicosity of the Kaiser as primarily a matter of the internal management of German public opinion in the years up to 1914.

The *casus belli* may mask underlying causes that reflect long-term shifts in the relative power of the opposing forces, perhaps as one develops economically or technologically more quickly than the other. Another way of looking at this is to claim that the wars are actually stimulated by economic conflict (the old Marxist approach) or technological conflict – whether a race to control resources or the opportunity given to one party by its overwhelming superiority. But the decline of historical determinism makes it clear that such factors cannot be considered alone, irrespective of the choices made by political and military elites.

The fact is, the outbreak of a war cannot be explained purely in terms of the strategic needs of generals, or the desires of politicians, or the demands of bankers, or the allure of armaments, or the hypocrisy of the priesthood, or the blindness of the people, or even the wickedness of human nature, important though all those may be. As Jeremy Black emphasises later in this book, full historical explanation also requires consideration of the cultural context, in particular the mindset and value systems of the leaderships of both parties. Some political systems are more likely to opt for war than others. The religious system that sustained the Aztec Empire in the 1500s saw war and sacrifice as a path to honour, and the entire Aztec social and economic system was built on the fighting of regular wars which would supply the prisoners whose blood sacrifice could feed the gods. Some interpretations of Islam promise paradise to those who sacrifice themselves in a holy war – bellicose policy is more likely to be found in a state where such interpretations predominate. Conversely, democracies like to believe they are notoriously reluctant to go to war, at least with one another.

No single explanation of war-making can embrace Aztec and Panzer, Mongol horde and Wellingtonian regiment. It is more fruitful to consider the circumstances that make rational men and women consider fighting to be a worthwhile option. Using hindsight to explain this can only diminish the weight of the original moment of decision.

Historians have always been fascinated by wars. Thucydides and Xenophon saw war as the result of political calculation and shifts in the balance of power, although both considered the wars they described as cultural clashes between two distinct and ultimately antagonistic world views – to Thucydides between the democratic Athenians and the conservative and oligarchic Spartans; to Xenophon between the imperial, oriental, tyrannical Persians and the federal, freedom-loving, nationalistic and decent Greeks.

To Roman historians Livy and Caesar, war was a natural

function of the state, something justified by the very successes in Roman arms that they chronicled. The historians and chroniclers of the Christian Middle Ages, led by the Venerable Bede, saw history as having a didactic meaning, tending to see the suffering caused by war as God's punishment for wickedness, and success in war as a sign of divine favour.

These two approaches, the realistic and the moralistic – supplemented by the structuralist approach that argues that wars are an inevitable result of fundamental contradictions in the system of power – have dominated discussion up to our own day. Plus, perhaps, the cock-up theory. While long-term causes were popular in the Marxist 1960s and 1970s, they have since fallen prey to revisionism: for example, the English Civil War was seen by Marxist historian Christopher Hill in the 1960s to have had long-term economic causes and deep intellectual roots in the transition from a feudal society to a commercial one, whereas today most historians, led by Conrad Russell, prefer to see the war as the result of short-term miscalculations and point out that no one foresaw it, even twelve months before hostilities broke out.

Not surprisingly, the wars that have seen the most debate over their outbreak are the two world wars of the twentieth century. While Fischer blamed the German high command for challenging British supremacy and destabilising the balance of power in Europe, others saw the First World War as resulting from a calculated risk by Germany that got out of hand; a third approach takes the focus away from Germany and blames the intellectual and cultural environment of Europe, while a fourth (recently argued by British historian Niall Ferguson) suggests the entire thing could have been avoided if the British foreign secretary had played his hand more subtly in the summer of 1914. Of course, these do not have to be mutually exclusive.

These arguments have a direct bearing on attitudes to the Treaty of Versailles, which itself is often seen as the contributory cause of the rise of Hitler and the return of war in 1939. Indeed, some historians (such as Michael Howard) prefer to consider the two wars part of a single conflict interrupted by a twenty-year truce. But the fact that the two major wars of the twentieth century were started by Germany led some to seek their origins in the bellicose character of the German nation – an approach adapted by Daniel

Goldhagen for his *Hitler's Willing Executioners*, a study of the place of anti-Semitism in German culture. For most, the Second World War was fought to end Hitler's plan of Continental domination and to avert the consequences of the Nazi–Soviet pact.

Fresh life has been breathed into all these questions by the war in Iraq, and historians have been as divided as any other group on its rights and wrongs. But they have probably been less noisy than in the debate on the 'war on terror' in the aftermath of the attack on the World Trade Center, when they debated the question of a historic 'clash of civilisations' between Islam and the West, as Samuel P. Huntington had argued. The typical historian's counter to Huntington's assertions was a sceptical one, with an appeal to caution and complexity, and attention to the specifics of when, where, who and how.

What wins wars

What wins wars?

Jeremy Black
Professor of history at the University of Exeter

? Historians used to emphasise the material aspects of war – specifically the quality and quantity of resources. Now, the focus is rather on strategic culture – how tasks are set and understood, how resources are used and how organisational issues are affected by social patterns and developments.

Old assumptions by historians that societies are driven merely by a search for efficiency and maximisation of force as they adapt their weaponry for war ignore the complex process by which interest in new weapons interacts with the desire for continuity. Responses by warring parties to firearms, for example, have varied over the years, with societies in Western Europe proving keener to rely on firearms than those in East and South Asia. This becomes easier to understand by considering the different tasks and possibilities that armies face at the actual time of going to war – when it is far from clear which weapons or tactics will be successful – rather than in terms of clear-cut military progress.

Cultural factors also play a role in responses to the trial of combat. Understanding loss and suffering, at both the level of ordinary soldiers and of societies as a whole, is far more culturally conditioned than emphasis on the sameness of battle might suggest, and variations in the willingness to suffer losses influence both military success and styles of combat, as differences in British war-making over the past century show.

Furthermore, war is not really about battle but

about attempts to impose will. Success in this involves far more than victory on the battlefield – that is just a precondition of a much more complex process. First, the defeated must be willing to accept the verdict of battle. This involves accommodation, if not acculturation – something that has been far from constant in different periods and places. Assimilating local religious cults, co-opting local elites and, possibly, today, offering the various inducements summarised as globalisation has been the most important means of achieving it. Thus military history becomes an aspect of total history; victory in war is best studied in terms of multiple political contexts.

As interaction of politics and strategy produces specific understandings of war and victory, these, in turn, shape responses to the prospect of future conflicts – not least because the major cause of aggressors deciding to go to war is a presumption of success. This means that cultural assumptions are crucial both before and after conflict. Indeed, the combat stage sits between these, as part of an ongoing process of warfare.

Aggressors rely on references to other conflicts to produce, or at least to sustain, this presumption of success. They scour histories of peoples and states to provide evidence of victory, while discussing other wars to suggest that the pattern of military history is clear. This entails conceptualising conflict in a way that deliberately minimises risk, and thus denies the nature of war and of its consequences: in practice, even if victory is likely, its results are far less so. For regimes considering conflict, military history has an important utilitarian goal: both encouraging people to fight for victory on the battlefield and securing a legacy of victory once the battle is over.

But military history should also be about underlining the precariousness of victory and the difficulties of translating it into lasting success. It is not that scholarship is inherently anti-war, but rather that subjecting conflict to scrutiny challenges the automatic consent for conflict that bellicose cultures are apt to assume and require.

In recent years, too much attention, relatively speaking, has been devoted to the 'revolution in military affairs' (RMA) discerned in American advances in information warfare and precision weaponry. In practice, it is not always the best armed who prevail, and there is no reason to assume that this situation will change, irrespective of technological developments; certainly, the Americans encountered difficulties in ensuring the outcome they sought after the overthrow of Saddam Hussein in Iraq. It is also important to note that the USA is the strongest and the exceptional military power, and is in some respects eccentric to the analysis of modern warfare. Indeed, expeditionary warfare is atypical; most conflict is within states, with militaries and paramilitaries being used to resist challenges to governments, whether authoritarian or democratic in character. In addition, military tasking involves fundamental issues of social organisation; internal policing, for example, is central to military purpose.

If war is seen not in terms of American tanks trundling towards Baghdad (tanks only charge in misleading popular histories) but of counter-insurgency operations in the jungles of Colombia, the rolling topography of south Armagh or the slums of the Gaza Strip, it is far from clear that winning means much more than the containment of problems. Historians need to address this civil dimension of warfare far more centrally, rather than considering it only in so far as it approximates to regular warfare between conventional forces. This is the type of emphasis usually given in histories of the American Civil War when, from the perspective of modern conflict, it is more instructive to consider those aspects of that war that approximated to guerrilla warfare, for example in Missouri, rather than the large-scale clashes in Virginia.

Finally, most war, both in the past and today,

occurs in the multiple environments grouped together as the non-West. This has become increasingly the case since 1945, although the Bosnia and Kosovo conflicts of the 1990s briefly suggested otherwise. Much writing on war is a matter of thinking within the box, with a particular tendency to treat the non-West as a primitive society in so far as it is mentioned. This is particularly absurd when so much conflict takes place in Africa, South Asia and Latin America. My emphasis on the non-West poses a challenge to the conventional approach to military history with its established cast of characters, events and ideas, but it is worth asking how pertinent that agenda is when general histories of war can ignore or underrate such large-scale conflicts as the Taipeng Rebellion or the Chinese Civil War.

There is a general problem with judging what is worthy of discussion in military history. Is it more important to emphasise Portuguese failures in Africa in the late seventeenth century – in the Zambesi Valley and at Mombasa – or Austrian successes in Hungary? And, if the latter, how much weight should then be put on Austrian reverses in the Austro-Ottoman war of 1737–9? How far are European gains in North America in the same period to be counterpointed by Dutch failure on Formosa (Taiwan), or Russian in the Amur Valley?

The lack of any obvious agenda for discussion is even more apparent prior to the period of Western power projection that began in the late fifteenth century. This activity at least provides a reason for justifying attention to the military history of states representing less than a quarter of the world's population, although the effectiveness of this power projection is generally exaggerated. Before the late fifteenth century, however, it is unclear why medieval European (and it tends to be Western European) warfare deserves the relative attention it receives. Its impact on warfare elsewhere was limited and, in scale, conflict in East and South Asia was more important. Even in the case of the

Middle East, the focus on the Crusades is misleading, not least because the extent of their success in part rested on the more long-lasting struggles between Islamic powers competing for dominance of the region. Furthermore, in terms of the dissemination of military technique, the impact of the Seljuk Turks and, subsequently, the Mongols was more significant than that of the Crusaders.

If we take a cultural approach to military history it is clear that not only the forms of war but even its fundamental principles have been subject to variety and change. This challenges the basic assumption of similarity hitherto underlying military history – an assumption that has condoned the way large periods of time (especially the Middle Ages) and much of the world (particularly sub-Saharan Africa, and east and South-East Asia) were ignored. Remove, however, the sense that military history is a matter of finding common themes or 'lessons', between Salamis and Trafalgar, or Alexander the Great and Wellington, and you are left with a more challenging subject, one, indeed, that may tell you something about war.

Wherever wars take place, understanding what wins them entails focusing on political, social and economic contexts, and on what caused the wars in the first place. Both within and between states, the politics of grievance are crucial in eliciting popular support for war. They provide a lightning rod for regional, ethnic, religious and class tensions, making it difficult to secure compromise. Resulting clashes are then remembered – as victory or grievance – in the collective memories of competing groups, and this helps to make it easier to persuade people to risk death. That is why we need to look at conflicts in terms of culture. While it is relatively easy to get people to kill others, it is less easy to persuade them to risk death over a long period. Despite the RMA fantasy of a one-sided banishment of the risk of casualties, the ability to persuade people to risk death and mutilation is a fundamental factor in what wins wars.

Further reading

Jeremy Black: *War: Past, Present and Future* (Sutton, 2000); *War in the New Century* (Continuum, 2001); *World War Two* (Routledge, 2003)

John Buckley: *Airpower in the Age of Total War* (Routledge, 1998)

Michael Howard: *The Invention of Peace* (Profile, 2000)

Lawrence Sondhaus: *Navies of Europe 1815–2000* (Longman, 2002).

Ever since there were wars to win, the question of what decides the victor has been a matter of far more than academic speculation. Rulers, generals and their chroniclers have always raked through the ashes of past conflicts to divine lessons for the future. Sometimes their thoughts were passed on to help the next generation, as well as to celebrate their own achievements.

Among the first to tackle the question was the Chinese strategist Sun Tzu. A contemporary of Confucius, Sun Tzu compiled a Swiss army knife of military theory in around 479 BC, known today as *The Art of War*. Covering a swathe of relevant topics, from deception to momentum to diplomacy, he drew conclusions from his own experiences to guide would-be leaders of men through the basics of waging a war. His work is peppered with such insights as 'do not start a war unless you can be sure you can win it' and 'in peace, prepare for war; in war, prepare for peace'.

In the West, the great Roman authority was the fourth-century writer Vegetius. His *On Warfare* was essentially a list of dos and don'ts, from how to select, train and equip soldiers, to how to fight battles and construct fortifications. Despite focusing solely on a Roman infantry army, Vegetius proved profoundly influential for more than a thousand years, alongside earlier classical writers, such as Greek second-century BC historian Polybius, the Roman military leader and dictator Julius Caesar (100–44 BC), and first-century strategist Frontinus, whose book *On Stratagems* gave examples of military stratagems for the use of officers. Medieval writers took their cues on how to win wars from Vegetius, while writing volumes about chivalrous behaviour and the legal aspects of conflict.

The great Renaissance scholar Niccolò Machiavelli (1469–1527) carved out a reputation as a military thinker with *The Art of War*. He also stressed the importance of warfare in *The Prince*, noting: 'A prince should therefore have no other aim or thought, never take up any other thing for his study, but war and its organisations and discipline.' He was an admirer of both Frontinus and Vegetius but his was no mere attempt at reviving classical military science. While Machiavelli discussed organisation, tactics and how to win battles, and pondered the impact of artillery on the strategic significance of fortifications, there is deeper analysis alongside this, and a bid to place war within its political and economic framework, if only to prepare the prince for the task ahead.

From the late seventeenth century, science and technology fired the imagination of the military writer. Both the Royal Society and the French Academie Royale des Sciences engaged in research projects intended to aid in the waging of war. Among the most influential figures was Sébastien le Prestre de Vauban (1633–1707), a French military engineer, who produced treatises on siege craft and fortresses, making science's new ideas and insights available to the soldier. Later, Jacques-Antoine-Hippolyte de Guibert (1743–1790), in his 1772 essay on tactics, looked to the successes of Frederick the Great, the eighteenth-century King of Prussia, who overcame remarkable odds to enlarge his kingdom.

Frederick's own *General Principles of Warfare*, which emphasised discipline and the organisation of professional armies, was circulated in secret among his generals before being published by the French in 1760. For Frederick, warfare was a contest of position, in which small gains were accumulated by forcing the enemy to move, through battles. Then came the French Revolution, and war was no longer a game for rulers. National self-consciousness was kindled, and universal military service produced citizen armies that made war more a clash of people. The German aristocrat Dietrich von Bulow, a contemporary of the revolution, reflected on this new age in *The Spirit of Modern Warfare* (1799).

Carl von Clausewitz's *On War* (1832) occupies a special place in military thinking. Although this posthumous volume is more often quoted than read, it was the first to truly grapple with the fundamentals of the subject. The Prussian officer, inspired by the Napoleonic Wars he witnessed, was succinct: 'War is nothing else than the continuation of state policy by different means.' War was a national act of violence, an instrument to achieve a specific objective that could only be achieved by disarming or overthrowing the enemy to force one's will upon them. At the heart of this struggle, according to Clausewitz's thesis, lay a particular 'decisive battle'.

In contrast to Clausewitz, the French military man Antoine Henri Jomini was not interested in philosophical problems. He too had witnessed the Napoleonic Wars and was clear that the purpose of war was to occupy the enemy's territory. In *The Art of War* (1838), Jomini comes up with practical advice that was to ingratiate him with generations of generals that followed. For him the key was to bring the greatest part of your forces to bear upon a lesser part of your enemy's forces at decisive areas in the theatre of war.

In 1890, the US naval strategist Alfred Thayer Mahan published *The Influence of Sea Power Upon History*, suggesting that domination of the sea, and in particular seaborne commerce, was the deciding factor in the outcome of England's long struggle with France. However, the detailed study of past conflicts by the German military historian Hans Delbruck in his influential four-volume *History of the Art of War* (1900) concluded that no single theory of strategy could be correct for every age, and that the aims of war could be more limited than annihilation of the enemy's forces.

In the wake of the First World War, new ideas emerged. The Italian air-power theorist Guilio Douhet argued in *Command of the Air* (1921) that successful offensives by surface forces were no longer feasible. The impossibility of mounting a successful defence against aerial assault left massive bombing attacks against the enemy's centres of population the only effective strategy. For Douhet, there was no longer a useful military distinction between combatants and non-combatants. The concept of what actually constitutes winning a war was changing rapidly.

The British military thinker Basil Liddell Hart in *Strategy: The Indirect Approach* (1927) became the leading exponent of using tanks to make deep penetrations into enemy territory. He stressed movement, surprise and flexibility, forcing the enemy to engage when and where the attacker wanted.

In the fledgling Soviet Union, advanced ideas about manoeuvre warfare were developed by Alexander Svechin, Mikhail Tukhachevsky and Victor Triandafillov, who advocated deep attack strategies in his *The Nature of the Operations of Modern Armies* (1929). Many of the leading Soviet military thinkers were old imperial officers whose innovations included combining air and land forces.

The dawn of the cold war appeared to change everything. For Bernard Brodie in *Strategy in the Missile Age* (1959) the bomb made war something that could not be won without catastrophic consequences. Hence deterrence became vital, while new ways of pursuing foreign policy goals had to be found. Thomas Schelling in *Arms and Influence* (1976) wrestled with the dilemma, drawing on game theory to devise new strategies.

The superpowers fought out their differences at a local level in countries such as Korea and Afghanistan, where people had to devise their own ways to wage war against a much more powerful enemy. In China, Mao Tse-tung in *On Guerrilla Warfare* (1937) advocated unorthodox strategies to give agrarian people a chance to win asymmetric wars against richer, urban opposition, while in Vietnam, General Vo Nguyen Giap developed guerrilla strategies that helped defeat first the French and later the Americans. This meant that counter-insurgency became increasingly important, and this was reflected in studies such as Robert Thompson's *Defeating Communist Insurgency: The Lessons of Malaya and Vietnam* (1966) and Frank Kitson's *Low Intensity Operations* (1971), which outlined ways in which the guerrilla threat could be tackled.

Strategic studies grew in popularity within academe from the Second World War onwards. One of the key volumes was *Makers of Modern Strategy: Military Thought from Machiavelli to Hitler* (1943) edited by Edward Mead Earle, which emerged from a seminar on American foreign policy in 1941. A similar volume, *Makers of Modern Strategy: From Machiavelli to the Nuclear Age* (1986), edited by Peter Paret, takes in the nuclear age and includes a chapter on the making of Soviet strategy by American National Security Adviser Condoleezza Rice.

Among recent leading academics to have studied warfare are the Oxford dons Michael Howard, who considers the interaction of war and society in *War in European History* (1976), and Hew Strachan, with the acclaimed volume *European Armies and the Conduct of War* (1983). In his three-volume *A History of Military Thought* (2001), Tel Aviv professor Azar Gat looks at the importance of political objectives in determining the use of force, and concludes that since most objectives are quite limited in scope, very few conflicts actually call for the overthrow of an enemy state – recent campaigns in Afghanistan and Iraq notwithstanding.

How do civilisations develop

How do civilisations develop?

Colin Renfrew
*Disney Professor Emeritus of Archaeology, and fellow of the
McDonald Institute for Archaeological Research,
University of Cambridge*

How did we as human beings come to be what we are? Just about every culture and every religion has its own creation myth, its own equivalent of the Book of Genesis. And today, modern science can actually offer us answers to parts of the question, which researchers have been investigating since the time of Charles Darwin. We now do know something from astronomers and cosmologists about the big bang and the origins of the universe. Moreover, we know from them, and from geologists, a good deal about the origins of the solar system and of the earth. Biologists can tell us about the origins of life and the evolution of species, and molecular geneticists have unravelled the genetic code of DNA. So too, after decades of research, particularly in Africa, primatologists and anthropologists can use the fossil record to offer a coherent account of the emergence of our own species from our hominid ancestors – the so-called 'human revolution'. But the most difficult thing of all to understand is human behaviour. After more than a century of study and archaeological research we still do not understand very clearly how the first civilisations arose in different parts of the world, and why they arose just where and when they did.

'The proper study of mankind is man,' as Alexander Pope observed, but our most remarkable achievement is still not very well understood. Evidence for the first complex societies – early state societies, centred upon great cities – exists across the world, from Rome, to Athens, to the splendours of ancient

Egypt. Then there are Nineveh, Nimrud, Babylon, the famous cities of Mesopotamia and their very early predecessors in the Sumerian sites of Ur and Uruk. In Mexico, the achievements of the classic Maya still dazzle the eye, and the great city of Teotihuacán in the Valley of Mexico, abandoned around AD 800, continues to astound us today as much as it astounded the Aztecs who ruled the area when Cortés reached Meso-America in 1519. The emergence of urban life in northern India and Pakistan before 2000 BC and the rise of Chinese civilisation around the same time are well established. So it is clear that in many different parts of the world civilisations did arise during the three or four millennia before the modern era, civilisations which we can recognise as in some ways similar, with their urban centres, their temples and palaces, their own writing systems and their state organisations.

Contrast that situation with the position of humankind some 20,000 years earlier. Then, all human societies were simply small groups, usually of no more than between twenty and forty people, living the nomad lives of hunters and scavengers for food. The transition that followed – from Stone Age hunter to urban dweller – can be documented in the archaeological record: we can dig up the campsites, the temples and the palaces; we can excavate the earliest village settlements in different parts of the world, and then the first tombs, and investigate the changing social organisation; we can seize upon the invention of writing in different continents, examine the origins of literacy and trace the development of centralised administration. But that still leaves the question of how and why these fundamental and radical changes occurred where and when they did. Why did they not occur everywhere much sooner? Or, indeed, why did they occur at all?

There is a paradox here, which I like to call the 'sapient paradox'. Most scientific attention has focused upon the emergence of our own species – of us – *Homo sapiens sapiens* in the standard nomenclature system.

The fossil record suggests that we evolved from our earlier hominid ancestors in Africa between 200,000 and 100,000 years ago. Modern molecular genetics shows us how little, in terms of DNA, we differ from our nearest ape relative, the chimpanzee. And recent DNA studies confirm that our species emerged in Africa and gradually spread out from there some 70,000 or 60,000 years ago, and over the succeeding millennia peopled the rest of the world, reaching Europe some 40,000 years ago. We can measure the increased cranial capacity of our early ancestors' skulls, and note the greater sophistication of the stone tools that they used. In southern France and northern Spain we can admire the paintings they made in the caves 30,000 years ago, with remarkably lifelike representations of the animals which they observed and hunted. We can assume that these humans of 30,000 or 40,000 years ago had the capacity for language, with most of the complexities of vocabulary and grammar that humans share today. Modern molecular genetics suggests that biologically, in terms of their physical and mental capacities – indeed in terms of their DNA – they were much like us. A newborn baby then and a newborn baby now would not be significantly different. Yet what I find so remarkable is that for nearly 30,000 years there was no immediately obvious and clearly significant change in the lifestyles of these early humans. To be sure, they spread out and peopled the earth. But they were still mobile hunters and scavengers, without permanent dwellings. Settled village farming life, with the formation of the first sedentary communities, did not begin in the Near East and Anatolia until around 9000 or 8000 BC. Comparable developments, with the inception of agriculture, took place in China and Meso-America and in other places, but rather later. How come, if the new *Homo sapiens* species was so clever, the development of settled farming life and the growth of cities, and indeed the rise of civilisation, did not occur much earlier? That is the paradox.

Recent work has given us some strong indications towards its resolution. One of the great triumphs of archaeology over the past forty years has been to locate and investigate worldwide those places where agriculture and early permanent village settlements first came about, and to study the domestication processes of the wild plant and animal species involved. Robert Braidwood, at prehistoric Jarmo in Iraq, and Kathleen Kenyon, at pre-pottery neolithic Jericho in Jordan, were pioneers in the study of agricultural origins, as was Richard MacNeish, in the Tehuacan Valley of Mexico. Recently, comparable work has been undertaken for rice cultivation in southern China. In many of these areas, settlement and food production allowed a population with craft specialisation to develop, with centralised government and urban formation following a millennium or two later. We know now that settled village farming was a precursor to urban life in these societies, and when and where it came about.

Gordon Childe was the first archaeologist to define and discuss the 'urban revolution' in the Old World, and Robert Adams first undertook a pioneering comparison of the processes of urban development in Mesopotamia and Meso-America. Since then, various key factors have been proposed for the urbanisation process: climatic change, population growth, irrigation, warfare, trade and the integrative influence of great religions have all been argued at one time or another. Thirty years ago, Kent Flannery wrote a challenging paper entitled 'The Cultural Evolution of Civilisations' in which he brought together a number of these ideas. He showed persuasively that no single factor taken in isolation could explain the rise of civilisation but that a multivariate approach was needed.

Recently, some scholars have criticised general formulations, such as those of Childe, Adams and Flannery, for lacking the fine detail necessary to account satisfactorily for any specific case. For, of course, each early civilisation, whether in the Old World or the New, was unique. It had its own environment, its own subsistence base, its own social system and its own particularities of belief. But the more you focus upon the specifics of a single instance, the more the explanatory power of effective generalisation is lost.

And some broad outlines are becoming clear. Climatic change must have played a major part in leading some hunter-gatherer societies towards food production; it seems inherently likely that food production would have been very difficult until the end of the last ice age, around 10,000 years ago. But the most startling recent discoveries have been in the Near East and Anatolia, where what appear to have been cult centres are seen to have developed – in some cases as early as, or earlier than, the first farming villages. Novel forms of symbolism, including religious ritual, played an important role around this time and may have preceded the development of settled society, and even encouraged its inception. This gives us, I think, a crucial clue. For it is the human capacity to use symbols and to develop abstract concepts, and then use them in practical ways, which is critical to the developments that did occur. 'Ownership' and 'property' are concrete examples. Until social groups lived in settled communities, kept flocks of animals and cultivated their fields, there was little scope for the notion of private property, or inheritance, or material wealth. These became crucial new realities in the world that developed.

So far there is no simple model, no equivalent of the double helix of molecular genetics to bring coherence and simplicity to the ever-increasing amount of data being collected on the development of civilisations. We are, however, beginning to see more clearly where the issues lie. They involve the development in early societies of new ways of understanding the world – of new concepts, involving, for instance, power and authority, which radically affected the way society was organised and what could be achieved. Writing, with all its potential for organisation, was one of these innovations. What is needed now is a new cognitive archaeology that will analyse more effectively the symbolic constructs – from the concept of the inheritance of property to more abstract notions of religion – that the creators of the first civilisations developed, and which in turn made further development possible.

Further reading

Steven Mithen: *After the Ice: A Global Human History 20,000–5000 BC* (Weidenfeld & Nicolson, 2003)

Nicholas Postgate: *Early Mesopotamia: Society and Economy at the Dawn of History* (Routledge, 1994)

Colin Renfrew: *Figuring It Out: The Parallel Visions of Artists and Archaeologists* (Thames & Hudson, 2003)

Colin Renfrew and Chris Scarre (eds): *Cognition and Material Culture: The Archaeology of Symbolic Storage* (McDonald Institute, 1998)

Chris Scarre and Brian Fagan: *Ancient Civilizations* (2nd edn, Prentice Hall, 2003).

Commentary by Stephen Phillips
Freelance writer based in the United States

The question of how our most characteristic modern pattern of social organisation arises penetrates to the heart of human historical experience. According to the dictionary definition, civilisation is an intellectually, culturally and materially developed state of social development, typically marked by notation forms, like writing, to record information and disseminate knowledge, and by the presence of complex social and political institutions.

Some of the first societies answering this description sprang up on rich agricultural land along rivers in North Africa, Central Asia and India, spanning – from the Nile in the west to the Ganges in the east – modern-day Egypt, Syria, Iran, Iraq and India. These cultures were distinguished from the itinerant farmers and hunter-gatherers that preceded them in the so-called fertile crescent, and that predominated elsewhere, by urban settlements and the achievement of enough agricultural surplus to support social and political structures like labour specialisation and kingship.

Though there was cross-fertilisation through trade, differences in the ways each culture organised themselves led historians to designate them separate civilisations – from east to west: ancient Egypt, Babylon, Sumer and Indus. Other civilisations that have been singled out for historical study include the Meso-American Mayas and Aztecs of Central America, the Incas in South America, and Greece and Rome in the Mediterranean basin.

For historians, civilisations must demonstrate a coherence and critical mass over time, Peter Stearns has observed in *Western Civilization in World History* (2003). During its expansion from 600 BC to AD 200, the Chinese Empire, for instance, featured a common language (Mandarin), centralised political and bureaucratic organs, and shared Confucian beliefs, Stearns noted. While some civilisations may be less politically unified, such as the modern West – generally referring to North America and Western Europe – they must display enduring common values and social and political patterns.

However, how civilisations develop has proved a vexed question, freighted with political baggage from the different contexts in which it has been posed over the years. Indeed, the term civilisations itself has become politically loaded, connoting the superiority of certain cultures, considered enlightened, refined and sophisticated, over those deemed primitive, savage and backward.

One of the first historians to broach the question straddled the classical civilisations of Greece and Rome. A Greek enslaved by the Roman Empire in 168 BC, Polybius declared his captors' meteoric rise a topic of burning importance. 'Can anyone . . . not . . . care to know by what means, and under what . . . polity, almost the whole of the inhabited world was conquered and brought under the dominion of . . . Rome . . . within 53 years?' Writing at the zenith of the Roman republic's fortunes, he ascribed its success to the synergy of democracy, aristocracy and monarchy.

The intellectual watershed of the Renaissance in Europe, with its revival of classical knowledge and artistic forms, bathed ancient Greece and Rome in a halcyon glow as cultural golden ages to which historians harked back reverentially. But during the Enlightenment of the seventeenth and eighteenth centuries this view began to be questioned.

The eighteenth-century French philosopher Voltaire declared that historians ought to broaden their horizons beyond the prevailing narrative tracing contemporary European greatness back to Graeco-Roman civilisation, where the Western 'rational spark' was supposedly first kindled. 'It's time to stop insulting all the other sects and nations as if they are appendages to the history of the Chosen People,' he asserted. US historians Paul K. Conkin and Roland N. Stromberg, writing in the 1970s, noted that his project was ultimately frustrated by what has been dubbed the 'rationalistic fallacy'. This is the assumption that people think alike – in this case like an Enlightenment intellectual – which led Voltaire to draw dubious analogies between the Chinese and European deists and Native Americans and natural philosophers.

Such ahistorical thinking was a pitfall Giambattista Vico (1668–1744) had warned of decades earlier in *The New Science*. Vico put a premium on cultivating empathy to understand other societies. The key to grasping the motivations of pre-rational people at the dawn of civilisation lay in studying their myths and metaphors, he contended.

Vico also put his own spin on the cyclical view, expounded by Polybius and others, of civilisations successively waxing (characterised by humility, a sense of awe and religious reverence, and hardiness) and waning (marked by decadence, corruption and dissolution before reversion to barbarism). With each turn of Vico's wheel it was onwards and upwards, and this conviction of fundamental progress was central to historical sensibilities during the Enlightenment and beyond. German philosopher Georg Wilhelm Friedrich Hegel (1770–1831) also located historical events within the ineluctable march of civilisation towards ultimate perfection.

This idea of historical progression resonated profoundly with Karl Marx. In Marx's secular scheme, the history of civilisation opens with primitive collectivism, succeeded by feudalism, then capitalism, before the exploited proletariat rises up and realises communism. However, Conkin and Stromberg have observed that Marxism too seems based on a reading of Graeco-Roman-Western history, and sits less easily with the history of other civilisations.

Blithe assumptions of progress – linear or cyclical – came unstuck with the horror of the First World War. The conflict brought forth such pessimistic tomes as German schoolmaster Oswald Spengler's *The Decline of the West* (1918–22). Others, like English historian Arnold Toynbee, saw humanity's redemption in a unitary world civilisation embracing a global religion. This was the utopian denouement Toynbee postulated in his ten-volume *A Study of History* (1934–54). Scanning some twenty-one civilisations, he saw the familiar alternating pattern of growth and decay, with religion the bridge between successive civilisations, note Paul Conkin and Roland Stromberg in *The Heritage and Challenge of History* (1971). Toynbee's work ranged itself against what he deplored as the creeping parochialism entering professional history, which had seen increasingly narrow specialisation and monograph-style studies.

However, reaction against broad sweeps and grand schemes was deep-seated in the wake of the twentieth-century atrocities committed in their name. Summing up the mistrust they now evoked, Karl Popper's 1957 critique of immutable, consistent laws in history, *The Poverty of Historicism*, was dedicated to the masses led to their deaths by bogus convictions that nations or races were divinely appointed.

Meanwhile, the study of ancient civilisations has been transformed by what has been dubbed the 'archaeological revolution'. This has been underway since Napoleon's 1798 invasion of Egypt, accompanied by a corps of two hundred scholars, who expropriated numerous ancient relics for study. Archaeology has helped to fill in blanks and open up new vistas of knowledge. It may be inferred from the discovery of a bronze axe, for instance, that the society that produced it had mastered subsistence (as the techniques entailed in its production were too complex to be juggled with rearing children and catching food) and engaged in trade (as the copper and tin of which bronze is composed typically needed to be imported).

Concerted study of ancient texts, together with the use of disciplines such as palaeontology, geology and zoology, has also increasingly been used to build a picture of ancient civilisations. Now, other fields are contributing too. Evolutionary biologist Jared Diamond's 1998 Pulitzer Prize-winning best-seller, *Guns, Germs and Steel*, for instance, brings to bear on the subject recent advances from molecular biology, plant and animal genetics, biogeography and linguistics. These suggest that the terrain, flora and species of Eurasia better lent themselves to farming, animal domestication and information flow than those of Africa and the Americas and that the more populous and complex cultures that emerged were more disease-resistant. Medical models have also been incorporated into the study of civilisations. One notable example is American historian William McNeill's 1977 tome, *Plagues and Peoples*, which showed how viruses carried by European settlers ravaged indigenous American civilisations like the Aztecs.

McNeill has been associated with the world history movement, which, while eschewing grand theorising, has tried to retain a feel for the big picture, and shed light on cultures hitherto overlooked. This emphasis may be the corrective British historian Geoffrey Barraclough called for in a 1956 essay, 'The Larger View of History', which declared that 'we should be better off if we could scrap our histories of Europe and free our minds from their myopic concentration on the West'. He added that this concentration 'while it may conceivably serve to harden our prejudices and fortify us in our belief in the superiority of our traditions and values, is liable to mislead us dangerously about . . . the world in which we live'. It is a view that meshes with postmodern emphases on highlighting previously marginal stories and off-centre analyses.

Meanwhile, globalisation has raised fears about the survival of contemporary non-Western civilisations amid cultural homogenisation associated with intensified international trade, multinational corporations and mass communication, Stearns has noted. In 1992, American scholar Francis Fukuyama put an optimistic spin on the trend in *The End of History and the Last Man,* hailing the 'emergence of a true global culture . . . centring around technologically driven economic growth and the capitalist social relations necessary to produce and sustain it'. Two recessions later, however, amid global unrest, there seems to be plenty of mileage left in the history of civilisations after all.

Why do religious and spiritual movements grow

Why do religious and spiritual movements grow?

Linda Woodhead
Head of department and senior lecturer in Christian studies,
Department of Religious Studies, Lancaster University

? Those who enjoy the spectacle of academics being wrong-footed will have been gratified by the general failure to predict the massive upsurge of religion that has taken place in many parts of the world since the 1970s. The rise of energetic forms of Islam, Hinduism, Buddhism and charismatic Christianity has exposed an embarrassing theoretical nakedness.

Some have blamed the failure on academics' long-standing preoccupation with secularity. The existence of a large and sophisticated body of theory about secularisation was of little help when it came to explaining the equally important process of sacralisation. But that is too easy. It is not that secularisation theory is wrong – one has only to consider the startling and relentless decline of churchgoing since the 1970s in most parts of Europe to see how right it was in its main predictions – it is just that secularisation theory can no longer claim to tell the whole story.

First, it is helpful to make a clear distinction between religion (the sacred as primarily a social matter) and spirituality (the sacred as primarily an individual matter).

If we begin with religion, and consider the historical record, it becomes clear that religions flourish when they are in alliance with earthly power. Such power may be political, economic or military. Ideally, it will be all three. The initiative for alliance may come from the religion or from the earthly power. Ideally, it will come from both, with both parties benefiting from their alliance.

Consider the spread of early Christianity. The key factor in its success was its alliance with the Roman Empire from the fourth century. Without this, its fate would probably have been similar to that of its rival world religion, Manichaeism, which failed to sustain political patronage, and was unable to consolidate its early gains.

Not that the adoption of Christianity as the official religion of empire was a fluke – any more than the adoption of Christianity as state religion by early modern European nations, or the ongoing alliance between Islam and various political formations were flukes. Successful alliance between sacred and secular power appears to depend on two main factors. First, the secular must have a need for the sacred. It must have a lack which religion can best supply (by acting as a force of national unity, legitimating the claims of a monarch, normalising social and gender inequalities, and so on). Second, there must be some homology between sacred and secular (the early Christian God bears a striking resemblance to the Roman emperor, for example, and religious ethics tend to support family values during periods when gender roles are disrupted in wider society).

This does not mean that religion only flourishes in alliance with weak powers. Even the strongest power may 'need' religion, as we see very clearly in the case of the USA today. As a popular bumper sticker puts it: 'God has blessed America. Now America bless God.' The question of which comes first, the conviction of 'chosenness' or the success of religion, is a classic chicken-and-egg conundrum. When imperial Britain was at the height of its power, it too experienced a period of intense Christianisation, and it too believed it was a nation chosen by God.

But there is another condition under which religion can also grow. For it does well not only when it is in alliance with earthly power, but also when it mobilises resistance to such power. Religion can flourish, for example, when it supports migrant identities within a wider, hostile culture (see Martin Scorsese's film *Gangs of New York*). It can flourish when it defends threatened national identities (consider Ireland and Poland). And it can flourish when it supports large-scale politico-cultural identities against a greater power (as in the case of post-colonial Islam facing the force of Western capitalism).

Thus the remarkable success of Islam in recent decades is best explained in terms of its ability both to ally itself with political power in various Islamic states *and* to serve as a defence and rallying point against the creeping power of the West, particularly the USA. Islam finds itself in the sweet spot where the two most propitious conditions for religious growth coincide.

Implicit in these remarks is the idea that the sacred is an independent form of power. Being relatively free-floating, it may ally itself with all sorts of things, not only earthly powers and political regimes. Indeed, individuals may also lay hold of such power, and in doing so turn religion into spirituality.

Not surprisingly, religions have powerful defences against the loss of their sacred monopoly. Individuals who claim a connection with sacred power can either be co-opted (usually as monks and nuns) or condemned (as mystics, magicians, witches and the demon-possessed). Recent papal denunciations of New Age spirituality indicate just how seriously the threat of spirituality is taken, and just how forcefully it is resisted. Spirituality is therefore most likely to grow when religion is not strong enough to control and contain it. And this is most likely to happen when religion is unable to form a strong alliance with earthly power.

Let me illustrate this by drawing attention to a highly unusual era: Europe, 1700–1900. What was so unusual was that the Christian churches managed to attain a massive cultural hegemony, more intensive and extensive than anything achieved before or since. Alliances with worldly power were a major factor, for

Christianity helped to smooth the transition to capitalist modernity by securing the precarious position of the middle classes, ameliorating the worst deprivations of industrial society, and pacifying women and workers. And, under the reign of ecclesiastical power, magic, superstition and spirituality went into steep decline. Subterranean spiritual currents like transcendentalism and theosophy were not only weak, but also self-conscious in their counter-cultural and anti-establishment stance.

The decline of magic that is often attributed to the triumph of science, I would therefore attribute to the triumph of confessional religion. When religion gradually lost its grip, as its role in securing the social order and providing education and welfare diminished, spirituality began to revive. But what was reborn was not identical with what had been in place before the early modern period. That had been a form of spirituality concerned with the attainment of what may be called 'objective goods' and 'external prosperity'. Improved technology, increased affluence and the development of a post-materialist society now gave rise to new forms of spirituality more concerned with 'subjective goods' and 'inner prosperity'. This was a new, personalised, form of magic, whose aim was to enchant not the world but the self.

In Europe then, where religion is now weak and alliance with worldly power is minimal, we would expect to find spirituality flourishing. And so we do: from Ireland to the former USSR, from Iceland to Italy. In the town of Kendal in Cumbria, where a team of us from Lancaster recently conducted an in-depth study of religion and spirituality aimed at assessing their relative weight, we found that if the growth of spirituality and the decline of organised religion continue at their current rates, the numbers involved in the former on a weekly basis will overtake the numbers involved in the latter on a weekly basis in about 2030.

Extending this framework further, one might also

predict that where religion is strong and is bolstered by alliance with earthly power, as in much of the Islamic world, individualised forms of spirituality (like some more traditional forms of Sufism) will be suffering. Again, the facts bear out the forecast.

But there is a third scenario as well: where religion is in loose alliance with worldly forms of power, but is not hegemonic. In this situation, we would expect to find the coexistence of both religion and spirituality. Yet again, the prediction is confirmed. To some extent we find this situation in the USA, where the churches become containers of ever more subjective forms of Christian spirituality. The more striking and important example, however, concerns the massive upsurge of charismatic Christianity in the southern hemisphere in recent decades.

For what we find in Latin America, Africa and parts of Asia is a highly deregulated form of the Christian religion, in which individuals take hold of the sacred, establishing their own priesthood and their own churches. Far from flowing in tightly regulated channels, the Spirit blows where it wills. And where it is received, it brings not only subjective healing, but also objective support and succour in making the difficult and costly transition to global capitalism. Like Islam, charismatic Christianity presents itself as post-colonial. And like Islam, though in a different way, it finds itself in a sweet spot for growth: able to draw on the resources of religion, while providing many of the benefits of spirituality.

I would argue, therefore, that religion is likely to flourish in alliance and/or defiance of earthly power, whereas spirituality is likely to flourish in the wake of such alliance. But I am equally keen to draw attention to the corresponding movement of secularisation which lies right at the heart of sacralisation: for when religion grows, spirituality tends to decline, and vice versa. There are certainly instances in history when the pendulum has paused at one or other end of its swing, but in the messiness of actuality it is more common to find it poised somewhere in between.

Further reading

Steve Bruce: *Politics and Religion* (Polity, 2003)

David Martin: *A General Theory of Secularization* (Blackwell, 1978)

Rodney Stark: *The Future of Religion* (University of California Press, 1985)

Charles Taylor: *Varieties of Religion Today* (Harvard University Press, 2002)

Linda Woodhead and Paul Heelas: *Religion in Modern Times* (Blackwell, 2000).

Commentary by Stephen Phillips
Freelance writer based in the United States

For much of history's existence as an intellectual discipline, the propagation of religion was scholars' sole subject of interest. For Christian and Muslim scholars, history told the tale of the triumphal march of the one true faith towards an apocalyptic reckoning with the Creator on Judgement Day, the coming of the Messiah, or some other date with destiny.

The etymology of the word religion, derived from the Latin term *religare*, meaning to tie together or bind, suggests how this unique relationship between history and religion arose. In classical understanding, religion bound together the human and the divine, and history delineated a divinely ordained chain of events. Accordingly, history was invested with the utmost cosmic significance as the unfurling of divine providence.

This eschatological scheme came to Christianity and Islam from Judaism. Paul Conkin and Roland Stromberg observed in *The Heritage and Challenge of History* (1971) that the ancient Hebrews couched their faith in a chronological consciousness, viewing themselves as a chosen people, exalted then cast down, awaiting the coming of a messiah to restore their kingdom or usher in a new, better, epoch.

Previous modes of thought had viewed the link between history and religion differently, Conkin and Stromberg noted. For ancient Indians, history was a remorseless cycle of creation and destruction, and Indian Hindu, Jainist and Buddhist religions aimed to transcend this cycle to attain nirvana. Ancient Egyptians, Sumerians and Babylonians recorded events and compiled genealogies, but the conviction that events were at the whim of capricious deities militated against attempts actually to analyse the past. Meanwhile, classical Greek studies, like Thucydides' *History of the Peloponnesian War*, tended to focus on discrete events, seeing the past and the present as directly comparable, rather than charting historical change. British philosopher of history R.G. Collingwood has remarked that the Greek belief in the unchanging essence of things was ahistorical. Conversely, for twentieth-century British historian F.M. Powicke, 'the Christian religion is a daily invitation to study history'.

For early Christian historians, there was only one religious or spiritual movement that mattered – Christianity – and it developed because it was God's will that it should. In his *Ecclesiastical History*, Eusebius of Caesarea (*c.*265–339), called the 'father of Church history', wrote a history of the world explicitly in terms of the development of Christianity from the Fall of Man to his own day. A century later, writing in the wake of the sack of Rome by the Visigoths in 410, St Augustine of Hippo took up the theme in *The City of God*, again giving history an all-encompassing Christian interpretation, and dismissing the pagan gods of Rome's heyday in the process.

His world view influenced historical writing for centuries, aided, in the Middle Ages, by the fact that scholarship was concentrated in the hands of the clergy. Monasteries became the primary repositories of learning and literary tradition. There, encouraging Christianity's progression became as much a purpose of historical scholarship as documenting it. Augustine and other early medieval historians stressed the importance of the Church's missionary role in spreading Christianity. But many also emphasised the role played by individuals. In the hands of monk scholars like the Venerable Bede (*c.*673–735), history was hagiography. The currency of such historical accounts was the lives of Christian saints. For Bede, such paragons of devotion and virtue served to inspire by example, and his *Ecclesiastical History of the English Peoples* may be seen as a proselytising tract.

Contemporary historians of the Crusades continued this tradition, with chroniclers such as Geoffroi de Villehardouin (*c.*1160–1212) ascribing the success of Western Christian armies against the infidel to key protagonists who displayed both faith in God and prowess in battle. For them, Christianity spread because God was on its side, but a strong army and, in particular, strong leadership, also helped. Arab chroniclers, such as Baha' al-Din Ibn Shaddad similarly described setbacks to the Christian armies in terms of heroes such as Saladin, who reconquered Jerusalem from the Franks at the time of the first Crusade.

The increased contact between East and West, and between Christianity and Islam, sparked by the Crusades, had an impact on all intellectual life, including the writing of history. No longer was the spread of Christianity the only story for Western scholars, not least because of splits within the Christian Church and growth in heresies. Rediscovery of texts from the pre-Christian classical era was also encouraging a more secular outlook.

This was a dominant feature of scholarship in the Renaissance. Niccolò Machiavelli (1469–1527) praised the ancient Romans for encouraging religion and religious institutions in order to inspire and intimidate the general population into maintaining civic order and achieving civic glory. In advocating the same for his own age, he did not mind what religion was encouraged – indeed, he believed that Christianity, by glorifying 'humble and contemplative men', had 'made the world weak'. Humanist scholars like Machiavelli were less interested in the spread of a particular religion and more preoccupied by the classical view of the purpose of history – that it should set moral examples.

The religious tenor of historical study nevertheless endured. While early eighteenth-century Enlightenment philosopher Giambattista Vico emphasised the man-made nature of history, he saw humans as unwitting agents of God's plan. An immanent God looms large in Georg Wilhelm Friedrich Hegel's nineteenth-century dialectical historical scheme too, with each era advancing divine providence though the clash of opposing ideas towards a brighter, better future. Even Leopold von Ranke (1795–1886), considered the father of modern historical research, reached for the hand of God where his powers of historical explanation failed him.

However, the emphasis on reason, and concern with universal principles, that dominated Enlightenment thinking in the seventeenth and eighteenth centuries, transformed attitudes to religion. One consequence was to push it into the private sphere. In *The Profession of Faith of the Savoyard Vicar*, Jean-Jacques Rousseau (1712–1778) suggested that true belief came from the heart, not the head, and appealed to a natural religion, without churches or scriptures. In the next century, increasing application of critical methods from empirical science, and the impact of Charles Darwin's theory of evolution, published in *On the Origin of Species* (1859), increased the tendency for such alternative explanations.

In *Elementary Forms of the Religious Life* (1912), Emile Durkheim (1858–1917) classified religion as 'primarily a system of ideas with which individuals represent to themselves the society of which they are members, and the obscure but intimate relations which they have with it'. Far from disparaging it, Durkheim considered religion integral to the social fabric, and was deeply troubled by loss of faith, coining the term 'anomie' for the moral vacuum and alienation that ensued. Elaborating on this, Max Weber (1864–1920) linked Protestantism, with its work ethic and tacit encouragement of acquisitiveness, to capitalism.

Such functional views of religion encouraged Western scholars to broaden their horizons beyond the Judaeo-Christian tradition. Weber noted that Confucianism and Hinduism appeared inimical to capitalism, while Durkheim studied Australian Aboriginal beliefs, arguing that it was possible to deduce universal truths from the simpler society that Aboriginals represented.

In a more recent comparison of religions, American sociologist Rodney Stark suggests that monotheistic religions, like Christianity, Islam and Judaism, with 'one true God', rather than a polytheistic pantheon or no God at all, seem to impart more fervour to disseminate their beliefs and convert unbelievers, while Buddhism, Taoism and Confucianism, all godless in essence, but embroidered with multiple deities in their popular forms, have coexisted for millennia in China, each lacking a god powerful enough to supplant the others.

Christian leadership of the United States, the rise of Islamic theocracies in the Middle East, resurgent Islam, Hinduism and Christianity, and the general groundswell of grass-roots spirituality have confounded predictions that advances in scientific understanding, the rise of consumer culture and other secular forces presage the demise of religion.

The spectre of renewed religiosity has led secularisation theories to be recast in terms of what Stark and his American colleague William Bainbridge have characterised as the inherent 'self-limiting' nature of the process. This thesis, also put forward by British historian Steve Bruce, holds that Churches tend to become steadily more 'respectable', aligning more closely with secular society as the price of wielding influence and advancing the worldly interests of their dominant cliques, but thereby compromising their popular appeal. Followers may simply lapse into non-observance, form their own sects, or defect to others that supply better religious compensators, such as stronger promises of rewards to come in the afterlife. This formula helps to explain the growing cleavage between the West, where traditional organised Christianity appears mired in inexorable decline, and the developing world, where it is altogether more vigorous. Philip Jenkins, author of *The Next Christendom* (2002), suggests that the fastest-growing types of Christianity in Africa, Latin America and Asia feature a less intellectually rarefied, omniscient, interventionist God – especially resonant to the poor and downtrodden.

Interest has also turned to the proliferation of 'New Age' groups in industrialised societies. The importance of forms of spirituality outside mainstream religion is something that Keith Thomas recognised in his 1971 book on sixteenth- and seventeenth-century England, *Religion and the Decline of Magic*. He suggested that alternative belief systems arose as a way to help relieve stress in adversity and explain misfortune. Writing in the 1990s, sociologist Wade Clark Roof argued that the smorgasbord of new creeds that emerged in the West in the late nineteenth century, and that have particularly flourished since the counter-cultural movement of the 1960s, shows that those straying from traditional religions are seeking fresh outlets for their sense of the sacred. Philosopher Charles Taylor has characterised this 'expressive individualism', ranging from esoteric movements like theosophy, to world-affirming movements like Transcendental Meditation, as a popular outcropping of the quest for authenticity that first surfaced among the elite intellectual and artistic participants of late eighteenth-century Romanticism.

Recent analyses by Linda Woodhead have connected the subjectivity of this do-it-yourself religious approach to relational, humanitarian, ecological, even cosmic concerns. Therefore, the development of spiritual movements is once more being placed at the heart of broader questions about the nature of the world.

How do intellectual movements begin

How do intellectual movements begin?

Anthony Pagden
*Distinguished professor of political science and history,
University of California, Los Angeles*

The American philosopher Richard Rorty once
said that philosophy – and, by implication, all
intellectual life – was a 'part of the conversation
which we are'. As with other conversations, this one
involves a number of speakers. Sometimes they agree
with one another, sometimes they disagree, sometimes
they all speak at once. Great intellectual movements
usually begin when there are a great many discordant
voices struggling to come to terms with immense
external changes, even if those changes are not always
immediately understood as such. And, as with all conversations, the directions in which they lead are generally more easily seen in retrospect.

The great intellectual transformations which
shaped Western intellectual life – the Renaissance, the
Enlightenment, modernism and now postmodernism
– were all identified as such by those who lived through
them. But it is only with hindsight that they have been
made into distinct 'movements' in the intellectual history of the West. All of these movements began as a
response to external changes, and an increasing dissatisfaction with the intellectual tools available to
explain them.

Take, for instance, what is loosely – and many
historians claim inaccurately – called the 'Scientific
Revolution', or – the term I prefer because it was used
at the time – the 'New Philosophy' of the seventeenth
century. This began when perceptive Europeans came
to realise that the two major upheavals of the sixteenth
century had robbed them of all certainty in the world

they had once enjoyed: the Reformation and the wars of religion that racked Europe from the mid sixteenth century until the 1640s had destroyed the religious authority of the Church; the discovery of America had undermined traditional accounts of human nature. If man could disagree so wildly over the meaning of God's words, and powerful, developed societies could exist which diverged so far from what in Europe was held to be natural, then perhaps, as the great French essayist Michel de Montaigne suggested, there were no universal truths but only local custom. The poet John Donne expressed it like this: ''Tis all in pieces, all coherence gone; All just supply, and all Relation: Prince, Subject, Father, Son, are things forgot.' And if that were the case, what basis could there now be for any kind of knowledge?

Such despair led to the revival of an ancient philosophical doctrine that, while it had never really vanished, had lain dormant for centuries: scepticism. The moderate sceptic believes that he has no grounds for understanding but his own senses. In such a world, the philosopher has to discard all prior knowledge, has to begin only with the raw material – the world itself – that lies before him. From this came a belief that the only kind of science had to be based on experiment, that the only kind of philosophy had to be one, as John Locke argued, which began with an account of the human sensations, or, as René Descartes claimed, with the simply irrefutable fact of thinking itself: *'cogito ergo sum'* – 'I think therefore I am.'

By the middle of the seventeenth century, all the older certainties, all the older sciences, had effectively been swept away. In particular, a view of the world that relied heavily upon theology – or what was broadly, and disparagingly, referred to as 'scholasticism' – had gone for good. People still believed that a divinity had created the universe but they now believed that the world – human and natural – was an independent entity that could only be understood by studying it directly.

This revolution had come about as a consequence of an extended conversation, across the whole of Europe: Thomas Hobbes talked to Descartes, as did Locke; Descartes talked to Galileo, as did Hobbes, and a host of less well-known thinkers sent letters back and forth across the Continent. The movement their conversation created, despite its immense complexity, had begun as an attempt to find the answer to a single question: what is knowledge? And, although that question had been asked over and over again in the preceding centuries, only when all the older methods of reaching an answer seemed to have been exhausted had it become obvious that a truly radical new set of philosophical methods would have to be devised. A new intellectual movement had thus begun.

Every intellectual movement is, however, like all real conversations, a continuous process. The New Philosophy of the seventeenth century, and the revolution in scientific thinking that accompanied it, would never have been possible without the changes in moral and social thinking which are associated with the humanism of the fifteenth century. For this had been the period which had witnessed not only the rediscovery of the sceptical writings which had inspired Montaigne and his successors, but also the creation of a more anthropocentric view of the universe, a view of man as the measure of all things.

The New Philosophy also paved the way for the great intellectual movement we call the Enlightenment. By the end of the seventeenth century, the religious wars were at an end, and the shock of new worlds had greatly diminished. The scepticism and rationalism that had inspired the New Philosophy now began to seem overly reductionist. Once the 'yoke of scholasticism' had been lifted by Descartes and his followers, said Jean d'Alembert – creator with Denis Diderot of the most characteristic Enlightenment project, the *Encyclopédie* – the way was open for a world in which all mankind would govern its actions by its reason alone.

But in the bleak world of the seventeenth century it had made sense to argue that humans only stayed together and behaved decently towards each other out of fear and a rational self-interest – what David Hume called 'the selfish philosophy'. What the Enlightenment added to the rationalism of its predecessors was the sense that humans shared not only reason but also a common identity that reached beyond mere calculation. Humans were not merely selfish; they were also compassionate and caring. And they were moral not, as the theologians had insisted, because God had ordered them to be so but because a moral disposition was a part of their being.

The great thinkers of the Enlightenment secularised the Christian God. In so doing they demolished all the older claims of family, king and country, all those hallowed customs, and God-made laws, by which humans had governed their lives. As the greatest of the eighteenth-century philosophers, Immanuel Kant, put it: 'To criticism everything must submit. Religion through its sanctity, and law-giving through its majesty, may seek to exempt themselves from it. But they then awaken just suspicion and cannot claim that sincere respect which reason accords only to that which has been able to sustain the test of free and open examination.' The allegiance of all humans could now only be to humanity itself.

I have chosen two closely linked moments in European history. But similar moments, and a similar interplay between external circumstances and the struggle to make sense of them, may be found at the origins of almost every subsequent intellectual movement. Romanticism was, in this way, a turning away from abstractions and from the cosmopolitanism and universalism of the Enlightenment in response to the nationalism that grew out of the French Revolution and the Napoleonic Wars. Once again, country, kin and custom became the focus of human life. Humanity was not an abstraction. Humans existed only as members of different nations or peoples, and each one of these was different. 'Frenchmen, Italians, Russians etc. I know,' wrote the embittered French conservative, Joseph de Maistre, 'I know, too, thanks to Montesquieu, that one can be a Persian. But as for man, I declare I have never met him in my life.'

Similarly, logical positivism and Freudian psychology in the early twentieth century can both be read as attempts to find deeply buried rational codes of meaning and conduct beneath the apparent disorder created by the First World War. Postmodernism, most of whose founders have lived through the horrors of the Second World War, is, in part, a rejection of the possibility of any kind of rational understanding whatsoever when faced by anything so inexplicable as the Holocaust. Human history is reducible to little more than our own self-descriptions, or, in Jacques Derrida's often quoted (and misquoted) phrase, 'there is nothing beyond the text'.

And since nothing can exist in a void, and a wholly new intellectual movement would be a wholly unintelligible one, each of these has drawn heavily on the past. Romanticism drew upon Scottish and Germanic folk tales as a way of capturing what it imagined to be the primitive heart of a nation. Twentieth-century rationalism revived – and, since it is by no means finished, continues to revive – some of the claims of the seventeenth-century New Philosophy. Postmodernism owes conflicting debts to both Kant and Hegel, and every age has unashamedly plundered the classical past.

Now, as we move into a new century with its own share of conflicts, I sense that the fascination with language and the insistence on the unreality of the world which has come to be called 'Postmodernism', and which has filled most of our more recent conversations, is fading. In its place, a new scientism is on the rise. Cognitive science, once linked to sociobiology, and stridently condemned as an intolerably inhuman form of reductionism, is slowly coming back. A new conversation, and with it a new intellectual movement, is about to begin – perhaps.

Further reading

Lisa Jardine: *Ingenious Pursuits: Building the Scientific Revolution* (Little, Brown, 1999)

Reinhart Koselleck: *Critique and Crisis: Enlightenment and the Pathogenesis of Modern Society* (Berg, 1988)

Margaret J. Osler (ed.): *Rethinking the Scientific Revolution* (Cambridge University Press, 2000)

Richard Rorty: *Philosophy and the Mirror of Nature* (Princeton University Press, 1979)

James Schmidt (ed.): *What is Enlightenment? Eighteenth-Century Answers and Twentieth-Century Questions* (University of California Press, 1996).

Commentary by Karen Gold
Freelance writer

Newton's apple, Darwin's *Beagle*, Brunelleschi's perspective: iconic discoveries lie at the heart of any storyteller's account of intellectual change. New ideas spring upon an individual genius, apparently from nowhere: blinding flashes of inspiration which formulate in a minute, a few days, at most a sea voyage, and which alter human perception for ever.

Professional historians have for a long time sidelined this '*eureka*' story, although they may exploit it – in books with titles like *It Started with Copernicus* (Howard Margolis) and *Charles Darwin: The Naturalist who Started a Scientific Revolution* (Cyril Aydon). But, at times, they too have located intellectual revolutions in the specificity of Great Men and Great Events.

For Jacob Burckhardt, publishing, in 1860, *The Civilisation of the Renaissance in Italy*, which would dominate Renaissance scholarship for more than fifty years, Western culture sprang reborn almost in a moment from the economic and cultural desolation of the Dark Ages. In the fifteenth-century northern Italian city states, man, in the particular form of individual geniuses like Benvenuto Cellini and Leonardo da Vinci, suddenly rediscovered his classical heritage, his political dignity and his central role in the universe.

An even more specific marker moment was identified by the French physicist and historian of science Pierre Duhem (1861–1916). Modern science was born, he argued, in 1277, with papal condemnation of the then popular Aristotelian philosophy that the universe could never be understood differently from the way it had been understood in the past.

Galileo, victim of papal authoritarianism, would have found ironic this theory of a papacy encouraging scientific hypothesis and progress. But Duhem suggested that the condemnation liberated future scientific thinkers, by enabling them to pursue their researches and frame their discoveries as steps forward in the comprehension of God's ultimate Creation rather than away from the belief that He created it.

Modern radical thinkers have added a new twist to this now unfashionable historical specificity of people, times and places.

Instead of focusing on famous men and events, they highlight the contribution of the unfamous, frequently women. Howard Zinn and Noam Chomsky, for example, tracing the intellectual and social spread of the twentieth-century peace movement, have both written about British activist Peggy Duff, general secretary of the Campaign for Nuclear Disarmament between 1958 and 1967. According to Chomsky, she was 'one of the people who really changed modern history . . . she belongs to the same category as . . . the unknown people who created the labour movements, or the other people who have mattered in history and are therefore unknown and forgotten'. By definition, these radical activists are portrayed as working against, rather than with, the cultural grain of their times.

Twentieth-century mainstream historians, widening the focus from individuals and peak events, preferred to adopt a looser idea of the soil from which new intellectual movements could spring: that of the world view identified by philosopher Wilhelm Dilthey (1833–1911). This was specific to a particular time and culture and often fertilised by particular events – the discovery of new lands, for example, or the fall of Constantinople, which brought classical literary texts back from the East into the West.

Later historians disputed both 'Great Men' and 'Spirit of the Age' explanations by emphasising the embarrassment of continuities between so-called new movements and the eras that preceded them. Harvard historian Charles Homer Haskins controversially called his 1927 book *The Renaissance of the 12th Century*, and identified most of the fifteenth-century Renaissance's characteristics within it. In the 1920s and 1930s French *annaliste* historians Marc Bloch and Fernand Braudel wrote of the long rhythms of history, identifying geography, economics and social structures as contributing far more to historical change than individual people or groups of events.

As historians took up longer-term perspectives on new ideas, they stepped into a new difficulty: Whiggism. Tracing the history of science in particular could easily become synonymous with tracing a red thread of truth as it gained adherents through the centuries. Even Herbert Butterfield, British identifier and arch critic of the Whig historical tradition, argued that, exceptionally, the history of science might need to be 'read backwards', and in his *Origins of Modern Science* (1949) did precisely that.

Yet for every step that ultimately boosted scientific progress there were numerous others leading only to blind alleys. Dutch historian Reijer Hooykaas, in *Religion and the Rise of Modern Science* (1972), wrote that scientific progress was neither linear, nor cumulative. The birth of the scientific method was not attributable to the observations of alchemists in their labs, he said. Instead, it developed with the dawning of popular scepticism that occurred when ordinary sailors realised that the supposedly authoritative maps they carried of the new worlds they were exploring were wrong.

Historians sceptical of dating the birth of modern culture too specifically make a similar point. Frances Yates, in *The Occult Philosophy in the Elizabethan Age* (1979), uncovered the magic and masonic networks which criss-crossed Europe throughout the supposedly humanistic Renaissance, putting an entirely different perspective on its intellectual context. John Hale, in *The Civilisation of Europe in the Renaissance* (1994), a deliberate nod to Burckhardt, emphasised that the fifteenth-century version of humanism was often far from humane: 'For some the Renaissance was a time of optimism and hope . . . For others it was characterised by wretchedness, increased rivalries, warfare and religious strife.'

Above all, Thomas Kuhn, in *The Structure of Scientific Revolutions* (1962), told a completely new story about intellectual movements, using the term 'paradigm' to signify a framework of ideas in which fresh starts were possible. Science was not so much a smooth arc of progress, he argued, as a series of separate paradigms, which, in turn, generated new problems to be solved over long periods of 'normal science'. Kuhn specifically criticised his predecessor Karl Popper, whose account of the hypothesis and testing process of scientific discovery, particularly in *The Logic of Scientific Discovery* (1935), has dominated the study of how scientific understanding changes. Popper's theory, said Kuhn, was too all-embracing: if every scientist in history had truly attempted to disprove their own theses, no science would have been left standing.

What Popper and Kuhn have in common is the story they tell of scientific discovery being dominated by conceptual change. New science comes about as a result of new ideas, they argue. Yet other historians have questioned this emphasis on concepts, pointing out that new movements may be prompted not initially by ideas but by the new tools that make those ideas conceivable. What would

Galileo have thought without his telescope? Or Brunelleschi achieved without his perspective-drawing machine?

And the impetus for new tools may have been nothing to do with intellectual enquiry, social historians such as Robert K. Merton (*Social Theory and Social Structure*, 1949), Steven Shapin (*The Scientific Revolution*, 1996) and Lisa Jardine (*Worldly Goods*, 1996, and *Ingenious Pursuits*, 1999) have argued. For example, Jardine emphasises the roles capitalist trade and empire played in developing new tools: 'There was this pressing need to have a clock that kept perfect time and a very precisely measured star chart of the heavens . . . When a group of men . . . need someone to tell them what the trajectory is of a body moving under an inverse square motion and constant velocity, Newton says "Well, it's an ellipse" and that is a piece of fundamental mathematics that only he could solve. But the piece of fundamental mathematics comes at the end of a story in which a dozen people, under the pressure of the urgent need to know where you are on the globe, have devised the question to ask.'

One difficulty with this argument, as other scholars have pointed out, is that in some cultures new intellectual movements have followed tools, and in other cultures the tools have been there but the movements have not. The fact that they can make this point is due to attempts to look beyond Eurocentric history. What Burckhardt labelled the Dark Ages were, as writers including Jardine have pointed out, the very reverse of dark in the Islamic world: the Abbasid Empire which spanned the eighth to thirteenth centuries was the intellectual powerhouse of the world, spreading and preserving not only Eastern mathematics, astronomy and medicine but also classical learning. Even the origins of classical learning itself have come into question, most controversially in Martin Bernal's *Black Athena* (1987), which argued that the intellectual roots of ancient Greece were not, as xenophobically attributed by nineteenth-century European historians, in Northern Indo-Europe, but instead in Semitic and Egyptian culture.

But the biggest geographic refocusing of the study of intellectual change has related to China. Joseph Needham's lifetime undertaking, *Science and Civilisation in China*, launched in 1954, revealed how, for example, Chinese mechanical clocks predated European ones by six centuries, while Chinese astronomers recorded sunspots more than a millennium before the Europeans did. While undermining the story of Western intellectual pre-eminence, Needham's huge study nevertheless fails to answer the question of why, when the Chinese had the tools, European, and subsequently American, science came to dominate the concepts.

Different scholars would variously cite economics, geography, politics and social structure in answering the question of why intellectual movements begin. But, for French historian and philosopher Michel Foucault, it would simply be the wrong question. We structure our questions according to the answers we want to get, he argued in *The Order of Things* (1966) and *The Archaeology of Knowledge* (1969). The history of ideas is a retrospective construct: we see intellectual movements in the times and places where we want to see them, and we write out alternative readings because they do not fit with the story we want to tell, the newness we want to perceive. In that sense, we have not come very far from the story of Newton's apple after all.

How does technology affect social change

How does technology affect social change?

Lisa Jardine

*Director, Arts and Humanities Research Council Centre for Editing
Lives and Letters, and Centenary Professor of Renaissance
Studies, Queen Mary College, University of London*

For Aristotle, the 'useful arts' completed and perfected what nature had begun, improving man's capacity to act upon the natural world, and enhancing the quality of human existence. Technology has been the catalyst for social change since before the Greek mathematician Archimedes demonstrated that water could be raised to irrigate parched ground above a stream by means of a continuous screw mechanism inside a flexible tube. Beginning in antiquity, what the seventeenth century later called 'mixed mathematics' created machines which freed men and women from back-breaking toil, and distributed the benefits of civilisation throughout the known world – from the simple lever and compound pulley system, to the vacuum cleaner and the washing machine.

For many people today, however, 'technology' is inescapably associated with 'biotechnology', and they have no hesitation in delivering a negative verdict on its contribution to altering our lives: new technology means genetic modification of natural plant species; genetically modified crops and foods are possibly irreversible changes to the environment and to tried-and-tested sources of nutrition on which we depend; so technology stands not for progress but for humankind's taking unacceptable long-term risks with the world we inhabit by tampering with it and playing God. The preface to a 2003 British Cabinet Office document on GM foods stated: 'The challenge for any government is to regulate the use of this new technology in a way that safeguards the public and our planet, commands public confidence, but also ensures that our society does not necessarily throw away the benefits science can provide. This is no easy task.'

Historically though, new technology has, on the whole, been seen as bringing obvious benefits to the least fortunate. The first applied scientific instrument invented by the young Sir Christopher Wren in the early 1650s, when his royalist family had been forced into exile in the farming community outside Oxford, was a piece of agro-technology. He devised a mechanised seed drill for sowing corn 'without waste'. Broadcast sowing by hand was back-breaking work, and much of the seed, scattered on the surface of the field, was lost; the drill opened up furrows to a uniform depth into which the seed was dropped mechanically. For Wren and his fellow members of the early Royal Society, as for many other inventive geniuses throughout history, technology meant first and foremost the route to rescue from sweated labour and want.

At the beginning of the seventeenth century, that great advocate of the advancement of learning, Francis Bacon, identified the printing press, gunpowder and the compass as the technological innovations which had enabled man to make the transition from the Middle Ages to modernity, based on 'natural philosophy' (science) and an enhanced understanding of nature. A century and a half later, Voltaire reiterated the claim, commending Bacon's prescience, and historians still agree that Bacon had astutely identified the key moment and technological forces and agents contributing to lasting social change.

There is surely no question about the impact of the printing press as a force for change. In the century following the invention of movable type in the 1450s, thousands of copies of the written word, inexpensively reproduced, came into the hands of ordinary people, enlarging the pool of those with access to the rich treasury of information drawn first from scripture and the classics, and subsequently from vernacular hand-books and practical manuals. Cheap, mass-produced books in every household encouraged literacy, which rapidly increased across Europe and beyond. Instead of gathering around the priest – privileged deliverer of divine truth orally to the faithful – each individual could now own and study the sacred text. Print led directly to freedom to think for oneself, to make up one's own mind on any question, and thereby forged the Western intellectual tradition. The technology of print may be said to have caused the Reformation (both Erasmus and Luther were masterly manipulators of the book), and ultimately to have contributed to the emancipation and equal treatment of women and ordinary people of all ethnic backgrounds and social classes.

Medical technology has further dramatically altered our expectations of life and longevity. From the syringe used to inject substances into the bloodstream and to carry out primitive blood transfusions as early as the seventeenth century, to the defibrillators, pace-makers and replacement valves now used with micro-surgery to repair a damaged heart, technology has allowed us to survive conditions that, until remarkably recently, would unquestionably have killed us. Full participation by women in professional and public life depends upon freely available contraception, allowing them the freedom to choose when and if they will give birth, overriding the natural rhythms of reproduction which had throughout history largely confined women to the domestic sphere. The current debate surrounding the provision of generic drugs for those suffering in the AIDS epidemic in Africa reminds us that pharmaceuticals and the development of chemical cures for resistant diseases are also part of the progressive world of new technology.

Historically, social change has been brought about gradually, in the wake of each life-altering technological innovation. Recently, however, the personal computer and the Internet, developing rapidly through the 1990s, have dramatically accelerated the speed at which information is distributed globally, and thereby the pace of social change across the globe. It is not surprising then that we are finding it difficult to judge whether the communications and data-processing boom is ultimately a force for good.

Indeed, at a certain point might this accelerated social change simply stall? Measures of social improvement based on the democratising of the means and processes of knowledge gathering, the ability to work from home, and immediate access to online learning can be used to argue that the lot of the individual has already been markedly improved by new information technology, and with it life in general. Read any issue of *New Scientist* and you can only believe that the world is moving at breakneck speed towards becoming a better place.

At the same time, however, the gap between the haves and the technologically disenfranchised has become a chasm. How many of those invited every day on the radio to 'log on to the BBC's website' have access to a modem, or even to a PC? For every one of us who now buys our plane, train and theatre tickets online, millions more are still waiting for electricity and clean running water. And not every technological innovation offers an obvious amelioration of the life of the average man or woman.

The growth of military technology, anticipated in Bacon's identification of gunpowder as one of the early modern period's agents for social change, is a clear case in point. Archimedes himself was killed in 212 BC, during the capture of Syracuse by the Romans in the Second Punic War, after his machines of war had failed to hold back the Roman army. By the fifteenth century, gunpowder had been harnessed to the construction of huge cannon, to produce the military hardware that brought down the supposedly impregnable walls of Constantinople in 1453 – delivering this gateway city to

Mehmed II at the very moment when the benign technology of printing was bringing the written Christian gospel to all of Europe. And although military technology – from Leonardo da Vinci's battering ram to heat-guided missiles – may have helped powerful nations to subdue their enemies, it has horrifically worsened the impact of war on non-combatants.

GM foods are a striking current example of a technological development about whose long-term consequences many of us are genuinely uncertain. For those, across whole continents, for whom getting enough to eat is the single most important item on their daily agenda, new biotechnology's drive to develop high-yield and blight-resistant crops, if successful, offers a promise of an improved way of life. Those in advanced Western societies whose produce is unthreatened by toxic blight, and for whom the additional waste associated with organic produce is not an issue, are in the luxury position of being able to reject the potentially irreversible changes of new biotechnology in favour of traditional agriculture. To the well fed of the developed world, the environmental risks seem overwhelmingly to negate any possible positive outcomes.

Indeed, one of the social changes to have resulted from technological advance – part of that acquired freedom to decide for ourselves which grew out of the technology of the printed book – is apparently a predisposition to reject unfamiliar technology, once an acceptable level of personal safety and comfort has been achieved for ourselves. In the absence of direct experience of life-threatening childhood illnesses, the level of MMR vaccination of children in Britain has fallen to its lowest level since it was introduced. Yet the official view is that 95 per cent of children should be immunised by their second birthday if we are not to return to a situation where the wider population is at serious risk from measles and mumps epidemics.

The history of technology has always been one of bold initiatives and of opportunities seized. The lesson of history seems to be that each new step in the onward march of technology should continue to be taken, cautiously but firmly, with each new challenge undertaken in the interests of the many, rather than for the satisfaction of those already safe, comfortably off and well fed.

Further reading

Jacob Bronowski: *Science and Human Values* (Hutchinson, 1961)

Lisa Jardine: *Worldly Goods: A New History of the Renaissance* (Macmillan, 1996); *Ingenious Pursuits: Building the Scientific Revolution* (Little, Brown, 1999)

Lewis Wolpert: *The Unnatural Nature of Science* (Faber & Faber, 1992).

Commentary by Steve Farrar
Writer on the Times Higher Education Supplement

For the people of the palaeolithic, the flint arrowhead was the key to a new world. With shared expertise and teamwork, small groups of hunters could use this technological innovation to get the food they needed with unprecedented efficiency.

Today, the Internet is also hailed as the key to a new world. With just a little tuition, a computer and global networks, vast numbers of individuals now find it simple to track down information and forge new communities that empower and enrich their lives.

Development of new tools and systems has a significant but complex impact on society. Yet explaining the nature of that relationship, through which our species has upgraded stone tools for silicon chips, has proved a challenge for historians since it became a matter for serious enquiry during the twentieth century. While it is a field profoundly linked to the history of science, it is also distinct. Where science seeks to explain and understand, technology exploits and fashions.

Overview examinations of the subject include the eight-volume *History of Technology* (1954–84), edited by Charles Singer. But historians have often preferred to concentrate on the development of specific technologies and their varying impacts on humanity. Carlo Cipolla investigates the technologies, such as gunpowder and compasses, that enabled Europeans to dominate the world in *Guns, Sails and Empires: Technological Innovation and the Early Phases of European Expansion 1400–1700* (1965), while Robert Maddin looks at the way metallurgy developed and shaped society in *The Beginning of the Use of Metals and Alloys* (1988), and E.J.W. Barber tracks the history of cloth in *Prehistoric Textiles* (1991). Alan Macfarlane, one of the contributors to this book, suggested in *The Glass Bathyscaphe* (2002), written with Gerry Martin, that glass was an important factor in the development of Western civilisation.

Communications technologies have proved of particular interest for historians, who depend on them for their work. Lucien Febvre and Henri-Jean Martin argue in *The Coming of the Book: The Impact of Printing* (1958) that the printing press crucially helped spread and popularise new ideas that were already emerging, while

Elizabeth Eisenstein in *The Printing Press as an Agent of Change* (1979) suggests that the print revolution prompted the Renaissance, the Reformation and the Scientific Revolution. Martin Campbell-Kelly and William Aspray explore the advent and impact of a more recent technology in *Computer: A History of the Information Machine* (1996).

Karl Marx (1818–1883) was one of the first to ponder the idea that human activity was influenced, or even determined, by its technological setting, and, although the question was very much a matter for twentieth-century debate, the Marxist school of thought on the history of technology and its impact on society continued to be influential. Its leading light was Edgar Zilsel, a German Jewish émigré to the US, who argued that science was born to artisan and intellectual parents, thrown together in the late Middle Ages as the burgeoning commercial classes pursued ways to improve technology. Hence capitalism was the midwife of modern technological progress that originated in the skills of Renaissance craftsmen.

Zilsel's suicide in 1944 cut short his career, while the collapse of communism saw his ideas thrown out with the Marxist bathwater. Recently, however, there have been moves made to revive Zilsel – or at least the kernel of his arguments – with Wolfgang Krohn and Diederick Raven collecting some of his key essays in *The Social Origins of Modern Science* (2003).

Post-war, Jacques Ellul, professor at Bordeaux University, took a firmly determinist line in *The Technological Society* (1954). Economic historian Robert Heilbroner's essay 'Do Machines Make History?', published in *Technology and Culture* in 1967, likewise argued that a particular society's technology imposed a specific pattern of social relations, though he noted that it was hard to gauge the degree to which certain sociological features were so formed.

Such ideas were developed further by Joseph Pitt, a scholar at Virginia Polytechnic Institute and State University, in his essay 'Discovery, Telescopes and Progress' in *New Directions in the Philosophy of Technology* (1995) and by Langdon Winner, whose book *The Whale and the Reactor: A Search for Limits in an Age of High Technology* (1986) sees in the concept an imperative 'to imagine and seek to build technical regimes compatible with freedom, social justice, and other key political ends'.

Otto Mayr, in *Authority, Liberty and Automatic Machinery in*

Early Modern Europe (1986), also explores the idea that technology sets limits on social and cultural forms. Mayr shows how machines were adopted by society as a symbol of authority and order. As absolutist regimes grew in early modern times, clockwork became a badge for those seeking to command a simplified European society, in which each element had its place in an overall ordered mechanism. As more liberal societies rose, the balance became the preferred emblem adopted in language and political thought.

The French philosopher Bruno Latour takes the interplay between society and science one step further. In *Laboratory Life: The Social Construction of Scientific Facts* (1979), written with Steve Woolgar, he concludes that scientific facts are not discovered but are constructed through social processes. Science is not an 'unveiling of some hidden truth behind things' but a heterogeneous project. The 'truths' that emerge from the laboratory, Latour insists, are shaped by immediate contingencies, such as departmental struggles over funding, the demands of a state armaments programme, cost of equipment or the influence of charismatic figures. Yet as these ideas gain support and become more solid, they often lose their links to the forces that helped to produce them. From his early work on the French microbiologist Louis Pasteur to more recent polemics such as *We Have Never Been Modern* (1993), Latour's arguments have helped spawn a whole way of thinking about technology and society, dubbed the actor network theory.

This theory has been formalised by Michel Callon, a professor at the Paris School of Mines, and John Law, director of Lancaster University's Centre for Science Studies. They have developed Latour's ideas by attempting to trace social connections between human, material and conceptual elements that produce new ideas and technology where they meet, highlighting the infrastructure that usually gets ignored in accounts of technological achievements.

Wiebe Bijker, chairman of the department of technology and society studies at the University of Maastricht, also stresses the importance of this infrastructure in his classic case study of the history of the bicycle, *The Social Construction of Technology*, edited by Bijker, Thomas Hughes and Trevor Pinch (1987). The book teases out the way social forces, properly focused, shape technological development: the bicycle started out in a great variety of shapes and sizes but the response of certain social groups helped constrain the design to the basic pattern familiar today.

Bijker aims to use the history of technology to empower people who often feel powerless to influence the modern technological world. He shows that a group that articulates its interest in the development of a particular technology can exert genuine influence, a message that has found particular resonance in the anti-GM campaigns.

In the UK, the study of the history of technology was for a long time subsumed by the study of the history of industrialisation. Until recently, few Britons would describe themselves as historians of technology. Among the most influential of those who did work in the field was Donald Cardwell, author of *Technology, Science and History* (1972). Cardwell's work was part of the British interest in industrialisation and focused on the place of science in the Industrial Revolution, on the links between science and technology as steam engines and factory machines became established. Cardwell was also a mischievous teller of tales, once convincing a television producer that German plans for the First World War invasion of Belgium included a scheme to unleash the *Sturmpanzerstrassenbahnwagenkorps* – the armoured tram car corps.

The British field has enjoyed a surge of interest in recent years. An influential group has emerged at Edinburgh University, with leading lights including Donald MacKenzie, professor of sociology, and his former student Andrew Pickering, now head of sociology at the University of Illinois at Urbana-Champaign. MacKenzie's work has involved studies of military technology, such as the development of missiles in *Inventing Accuracy: A Historical Sociology of Nuclear Missile Guidance* (1990). In *The Mangle of Practice: Time, Agency and Science* (1995), Pickering explores the building of the particle physics bubble chamber, among other innovations, to show how technology emerges from human interaction with a host of other factors – social, technological, conceptual and natural.

How do cultural booms happen

How do cultural booms happen?

Ludmilla Jordanova
Professor of modern history, King's College, London

? It is commonly assumed that cultural booms
happen, that there are periods of cultural intensity that historians ought to get to grips with. But
almost every element here is problematic. What counts
as a cultural boom? What do we mean by culture? What
would a satisfying explanation look like? Is the idea of a
boom helpful? Since 'boom' has strong economic associations, one route might be to consider exceptionally
high levels of cultural production and consumption,
although their measurement is hardly straightforward.
Phenomena that are culturally significant are rarely primarily quantitative, although I should confess that the
first example that sprang to my mind was Beatlemania,
where the numbers of records sold and the size of the
crowds would indeed be easy ways of reckoning the
impact of the pop group. But the cultural boom here
must, surely, be the sixties rather than the popularity of
one particular group. And that much mythologised
decade is indeed frequently presented in terms that
combine economic boom with cultural blossoming.

It is widely conceded now that the simple distinction between popular and elite culture is not terribly
helpful. So when we evoke culture in relation to the
1960s, a mixture of fashion, art, music, architecture,
design and retailing comes readily to mind. Yes, we
believe there was, in a number of ways, more of just
about everything at that time. But, and this is the crucial point, two other phenomena are involved. A fresh
consciousness is attributed to the 1960s – claims about
changing behaviour and mentalities are frequently

made. Furthermore, the changes were registered at the time, so that some people at least possessed a self-awareness of being in, perhaps also of making, a time of cultural boom.

We might say then that cultural booms involve the prominence, both in people's minds and in a range of artefacts, of something that is immediate, fresh, significant. So how do they come about? We can, I think, describe in considerable detail the processes whereby ideas, images and objects are disseminated, and in retrospect it is sometimes apparent why one thing is taken up rather than another, but further explanation is difficult to find. There are vogues, fashions and shifts in taste, and many historians have charted them in one form or another, but generally this involves noting that they are vogues, fashions and trends, rather than accounting for the how and why of them.

Whether we see cultural booms in terms of surges of excellence – late nineteenth-century Paris or early twentieth-century Vienna, for example – or in terms of explosions of popular enthusiasm, they always involve two phenomena. First, they involve ideas, which I would define broadly enough to include preferences for colours, motifs, styles. (Finding psychedelic patterns alluring depends on ideas, including some quite elaborate ones about the nature of the mind and its stimulation.) Second, they involve groups – the very notion of a cultural boom implies collective responses of some kind. It is revealing that there are expressions – *Zeitgeist*, in the air – to evoke just this point without indicating at all how and why these things occur.

Accounting for causes when ideas are involved strikes me as particularly difficult. Take the following example. Scholars from many different disciplines have noted a marked shift around the middle of the eighteenth century, in several geographical areas, in attitudes to children, motherhood, breastfeeding and familial intimacy. There is considerable evidence to suggest that the shifts occurred fairly fast, roughly between the 1740s and 1760s. This shift in attitude was accompanied by changes in culture, such as sentimental representations, in both verbal and visual forms, of mothers and breastfeeding. It is common for historians to invoke the name of Rousseau, and in particular *Émile* (1762), to account for these quite general changes in art, literature and in social practices. I am sceptical about the adequacy of this explanation. The chronology does not really work, in that sentimentalising children and mothers started before *Émile* was published, and certainly before it had a chance to make an impact. Furthermore, is it plausible to give such weight to one book? While there can never be a general answer – each case needs to be considered on its own terms – it is still worth asking the question. It forces, on the one hand, a careful consideration of publishing, distribution and readership, and, on the other, an assessment of the vexed notion of 'influence'.

Naturally, there are instances where it is possible to track in a precise manner the impact of ideas, products and people upon each other. The notion of networks can also be handy in charting the ways in which ideas spread and gain currency. But this is to remain at the level of description. We are still faced with accounting for choices, and also for the emotional and intellectual intensity that the phrase 'cultural booms' implies, since these can never be understood purely quantitatively.

Is a cultural boom something that involves high achievement – the most distinguished attainments in elaborate, refined, technically demanding areas – or should the Posh and Becks phenomenon also be regarded as a cultural boom? Is the ubiquity of an idea, or a person, one definition of cultural boom? Yet ubiquity is itself far from self-evident. It changes as forms of culture themselves change – in the age of the Internet, ubiquity can be of a quite distinctive kind. Moreover, high levels of cultural distinction, whether designated as such retrospectively or at the time, do not easily translate into ubiquity, hence judgements about cultural quality would seem unavoidable.

Many historians have examined early twentieth-century Vienna as the place that gave birth to important, influential, transforming forms of culture. It is widely held, with justification, that psychoanalysis, to take just one example, has changed for ever the general understanding of human beings, whether one 'agrees' with or 'likes' it or not. Readers may be irritated by this use of scare quotes, but they conveniently signal a vital point. As well as judgements about quality, cultural booms frequently provoke intense emotional reactions.

Recognising such complexities and dealing with them responsibly are central to the historian's craft. So it should be possible, I contend, to give an account of the 'Foucault boom' among academics since the 1970s that is judicious, regardless of what one's feelings about Michel Foucault are. In other words, a measure of critical distance is essential, and it can be underwritten by relatively impersonal assessments of impact. Perhaps this is where – finally – citation indices come into their own. We can examine numbers of editions, translations, copies sold, conferences devoted to a given theme, for Foucault as for Rousseau, or Dr Spock.

Yet such information, like hits on a website, numbers of records or postcards sold, seems inherently limited. In its way, it is as limited as invocations of a *Zeitgeist* or claims about something being 'timely'. It fails to grasp the very quality that makes a phenomenon into a boom. How do we name this quality?

I simply do not know the answer. Historians have given more or less persuasive accounts of cultural booms. There are an almost infinite number of ways in which such accounts could be cast – in terms of consumption, consumerism and marketing, in terms of desire, in terms of specific needs, in terms of taste and fashion, in terms of genius, or happenstance, or patronage, or even oppressive regimes, which are sometimes claimed to stimulate creativity.

It is precisely in areas such as these that historians meet their greatest challenges. I happen not to find the notion of boom especially helpful. Yet there is no doubt that forms of culture, however we define it, operate with different kinds and levels of intensity, that ideas and representations capture the collective imagination to varying degrees, that some cultural movements simply are more significant and insinuating than others. So the challenges remain. I have noted that historians seek to map forms of culture and that they argue about the nature of culture itself. They will go on doing so, even while they worry at how to study and convey the distinctive characteristics of those parts of culture that grip the collective mind most tightly. One phenomenon they may care to consider is the recent history boom.

Further reading

G.J. Barker-Benfield: *The Culture of Sensibility: Sex and Society in Eighteenth-Century Britain* (University of Chicago Press, 1992)

Maxine Berg: *The Age of Manufactures, 1700–1820: Industry, Innovation and Work in Britain* (2nd edn. Routledge, 1994)

Ludmilla Jordanova: *History in Practice* (Hodder Arnold, 2000, 2nd edn. 2005)

Arthur Marwick: *The Sixties. Cultural Revolution in Britain, France, Italy and the United States* (Oxford University Press, 1998)

Simon Schama: *The Embarrassment of Riches: An Interpretation of Dutch Culture in the Golden Age* (Knopf, 1987)

C. Schorske: *Fin-de-siècle Vienna: Politics and Culture* (Knopf, 1979).

It was as if a demoniac energy had possessed London. The capital of what had once been one of Europe's backwaters experienced, between 1570 and 1620, a sudden theatrical explosion unlike anything the world had seen.

The traveller Fynes Moryson wrote in his *Itinerary* of 1617: 'There be, in my opinion, more Playes in London than in all the partes of the worlde I have seene, so doe these players or Comedians excell all other in the worlde.'

It had really started in the spring of 1576 when James Burbage built London's first purpose-built home for drama at Shoreditch – called straightforwardly, the 'Theatre'. By 1620, nearly a dozen new professional theatres had followed Burbage's lead as London was overtaken by a mania for the stage encompassing everybody from the haughtiest courtly gentlemen to the rowdiest apprentice boy.

More than eight hundred new plays were performed on London stages between the opening of the Shoreditch theatre and the death of Shakespeare forty years later. Shakespeare was just one of a new breed of phenomenally productive professional playwrights, including Christopher Marlowe and Ben Jonson. Beyond the stage, England was also enjoying the new authorised version of the Bible and the poetry of Donne and Spenser.

C.S. Lewis observed that nothing in the England before 1570 'would have enabled the sharpest observer to foresee this transformation'. He said: 'The mid-century is an earnest, heavy-handed, commonplace age: a drab age. Then, in the last quarter of the century the unpredictable happens. With startling suddenness we ascend. Fantasy, conceit, paradox, colour, incantation return. Youth returns.'

If ever there was one, this was a 'cultural boom'. But, according to the city planner and historian Peter Hall, such a surge of creativity is not unique. Hall's *Cities in Civilisation* (1998) exhaustively examines more than a dozen cultural, technical and scientific 'golden ages' including fifth-century BC Athens (Protagoras, Hippocrates, Socrates, Plato and Aristotle; Greek drama, sculpture and architecture), Renaissance Florence, Vienna between 1780 and 1910

(Mahler, Schoenberg, Freud, Wittgenstein, Klimt), Los Angeles during the heyday of Hollywood, and Memphis in the eight years between 1948 and 1956 which saw the birth of rock and roll.

For Hall, cultural history is not a stately procession in which all periods and places take an equal part, but a series of lung-burning sprints, punctuated by longer periods of relative idleness. Arthur Koestler made the point in *The Act of Creation* in 1964: 'It is easy to match, in the history of every culture or country, the relatively brief periods of rapid cumulative advances with much longer periods of stagnation, one-sidedness, mannerism and estrangement from reality.'

But how are the flames of these extraordinary booms sparked? And how are they doused? Hall's study, published in 1998, notes a surprising lack of analysis of the question among his predecessors: 'If we now pay a precautionary visit to the map room, we shall find the shelves curiously ill stocked: in search for a theory of the culturally creative city, we discover surprisingly little that is either relevant or useful.'

Perhaps the most imposing set of volumes on these bare shelves is Arnold Hauser's voluminous *Social History of Art* (1951). Hauser's Marxist tour de force is light on theory, preferring to communicate its analysis through specific case studies, but its overall approach is clear enough: cultural creativity is determined by changes in economic modes of production. Hauser's is not a crude determinist analysis, and individual artists are appreciated for their distinctive contributions. However, his Marxist starting point, which seeks to understand artists as puppets of broad historical and economic forces, makes his work, and that of lesser Marxist cultural historians, unrewarding for someone trying to understand what sparks particularly intense cultural activity in certain periods and locations. Hauser's broad brush is simply not designed to paint a detailed picture of why Vienna in the early 1900s, for instance, was so particularly creative.

Much traditional art history, on the other hand, has focused on the creativity of individual artists. For Giorgio Vasari, whose *Lives of the Painters, Sculptors and Architects* (1550) pioneered the discipline, the central focus is on the 'genius' of the great masters like Michelangelo and Raphael, and it is from Vasari's example that much later biography of great cultural figures has found its inspiration. Although such biographical approaches will often carefully describe the various social pressures and influences on an artist, the essential 'cause' of the creativity is assumed to lie within the individual.

One of the most influential historians to challenge this approach, by identifying the forces behind a surge in the number of creative individuals at a particular time, was Jacob Burckhardt. His *The Civilization of the Renaissance in Italy* (1860) traced the transition from medieval society to the boom in individual creativity that appeared in fourteenth-century Italy. For him, it was a time and place when people who, influenced by the teachings of the Church and traditional prejudices, had previously recognised themselves only as a member of a race, nation, party, corporation or family, suddenly developed both an objective perception of the world and a subjective self-consciousness.

More recent theorists are now also beginning to ask why, if genius is fairly evenly spread across populations and generations – much like the distribution of extreme foot sizes – do some generations leave such a big cultural footprint?

The Chicago University psychologist Mihály Csikszentmihályi wrote in 1990 that he had started his research into creativity a quarter of a century before, looking for the personality traits of particularly creative individuals, but had been disappointed. 'Being trained as a psychologist, I came to this conclusion reluctantly; but now I am convinced that it is not possible to even think about creativity, let alone measure it, without taking into account the parameters of the cultural . . . domain in which the creative activity takes place.'

Looking at Renaissance Florence, for instance, Csikszentmihályi stressed the influence on the artistic community of exceptionally supportive patronage and the cross-fertilisation from discoveries by humanist scholars in the same period: 'The dome that Brunelleschi designed for the Florentine cathedral in 1420, which is generally considered one of the most brilliant achievements of the Renaissance, was made possible by the recently completed studies of how the Romans built the dome of the Pantheon. It does not make sense to say that these developments . . . "facilitated" or "influenced" the creativity of a Donatello or a Brunelleschi. They were just as essential to it as anything these individuals brought to the process.'

Csikszentmihályi is just one of a number of thinkers from a variety of backgrounds to focus on the 'cultural domain'. The Swedish geographer Gunnar Törnquist talks about the importance of the 'creative milieu'. The University of California psychologist David M. Harrington, stressing the unpredictable and organic nature of these environments, compares them to 'creative eco-systems'. All these writers have begun to see the social and physical environments that produce great cultural activity as worthy of study in themselves.

Hall is definite about one common characteristic of all such environments. Every 'golden age', he says, has always sprung from a city. It has been in such urban environments that creative individuals have been able to access the fast communications that allow them to connect with potential consumers of their work and cross-fertilise their thinking with other creative people's ideas (although, he admits, modern communications such as the Internet and global markets might upset his generalisation in the future).

Of course, most cities, most of the time, have produced chronic traffic and waste-disposal problems more reliably than extraordinary creativity. So what extra spark is needed? Hall's detailed study of Shakespeare's London shows that, like Florence at the start of the Renaissance, it was experiencing an economic boom and the birth of a new class of affluent consumers with money to spend. John Maynard Keynes, in his *Treatise on Money*, commented: 'We were just in a position to afford Shakespeare at the moment when he presented himself.'

However, it would be wrong to associate cultural innovation solely with wealthy consumers. Francis Haskell pointed out in his 1963 study of Italian baroque painting that patrons could hardly have been more generous or tolerant during that period. Achievements, however, were disappointing compared to other parts of Europe. 'Unorthodoxy was killed with kindness,' Haskell commented.

Equally, some cultural booms seem partly to result from economic restrictions. 'Manga', the peculiarly rich Japanese cartoon tradition that is beginning to have a pervasive influence on popular graphic culture across the globe, was, according to Frederik L. Shodt's 1983 study of the phenomenon, greatly enriched by post-war Japan's inability to finance feature films. Innovative visual artists expressed themselves in pulp comic books rather than on the big screen. Hall says that the Memphis that gave birth to rock and roll was 'miserably impoverished' and some of its most creative citizens were its poorest and most oppressed.

What often does seem to be present, according to Hall, is what we might call 'culture-preneurship'. Even in creative milieux not dominated by a mass consumer market, such as Renaissance Florence, innovative patrons have tended to play a decisive 'entrepreneurial' role by seeing the opportunity of converting artists' creativity into, not money, but power or prestige. In cities like Elizabethan London, the motivation was a more straightforward pursuit of lucre. It was pioneering theatre managers like James Burbage who created what turned out to be a fertile link between writers like Shakespeare and the London theatrical audience. Without them we might have had some delicate sonnets and courtly dramas but would we have had *Macbeth*? In Memphis, the Sun Record label played a vital role in creating the new music, as did Factory Records in the Manchester music scene of the 1980s.

Yet creative environments are mercurial – not only in terms of how creative industries and their audiences interact, but also in the way creative individuals share ideas. Törnquist highlights the importance of a flourishing café culture in Vienna between 1880 and 1930 in that city's extraordinary productivity.

Even more unpredictable is how one period's creativity will interact with its posterity. Csikszentmihályi's concept of the 'cultural domain' stresses that all 'golden ages' are understood through the value systems of the generations that follow them, and whether a period's cultural activity will be gilded in this way depends largely on the preoccupations of those generations. Csikszentmihályi argues, for instance, that 'Rembrant's "creativity" was constructed after his death by art historians' and that, had those historians developed a different taste, 'it is very likely that Rembrandt would have stayed in relative obscurity'. Similarly, the foundation of Shakespeare's current reputation was built on his appeal to the nationalist concerns of the Victorian theatre.

Another Swede, Anders Karlquist, has pointed out that 'uncertainty and ambivalence' is fundamental not just to the social interactions that can help inspire new thought but to the processes of that thought itself.

'It is perhaps no accident that a creative process often starts with the scribbling down of ideas on a napkin or on the table cloth,' Karlquist writes. 'The napkin is not only a practical device but it is also a representation of the fuzziness and playfulness of the situation. [It is on] the edge of chaos.'

How does private life affect public life

How does private life affect public life?

Sheila Rowbotham

Professor in gender and labour history, sociology department,
Manchester University

A well-thumbed history book of Britain called *Our Island Story*, which I read as a child, contained pictures of a young Victoria in her nightgown and shawl hearing the news that she had become Queen, and of Elizabeth I dancing alone in an elaborate dress, pretending she did not see the foreign diplomat peeping at her from the balcony. More troubling was the picture of the religious martyr being burned at the stake. Not yet ten, I worried over the pain of such a death. These personal stories tended to fade from the history I learned as I grew older. I assumed then that it was because I was growing up, but it was also because social and economic history was coming to the fore.

Recently, the television history presented by Simon Schama and David Starkey has returned to the narrative form I encountered as a child. These histories are more sophisticated of course but from their differing perspectives follow the same mix of personal anecdote and action on the public stage. My unease about this kind of history is not because private and public lives are represented as interwoven – clearly Henry's desire for Anne Boleyn did have public consequences and Mary's character *was* to affect the fate of Scotland. It is rather that an unproblematic focus on the great returns us to a history in which the great mass of human beings are again constituted as the chorus, chanting 'rhubarb, rhubarb' in the background, stripped not only of a public role but of subjectivity.

During the nineteenth and early twentieth centuries, the labour movement challenged the scope of history and demanded that it should be enlarged to include the actions and everyday life of working-class people. The labour history that emerged from this was to be influenced by both labourism and Marxism. Its focus on the creation of cooperatives or trade unions, on working-class movements and institutions, along with conditions at work, expanded the topics acknowledged as 'history'. However, it tended to eschew the private. One reason was that as an 'oppositional culture', distinct from mainstream history writing, the history of the working class was open to attack from more conservative historians, making its exponents protective and defensive about the good name of its well-known figures. Thus the labourist tradition kept quiet about Keir Hardie's affair with Sylvia Pankhurst, just as the Communist Party was reluctant to admit that Karl Marx had an illegitimate son, Freddy, with the family servant. Even in 2003, this latter historical fact caused amazement to some South Korean left-wing trade unionists visiting Britain to investigate working-class culture. The other reason was the tendency in Marxism to prioritise the public over the private. The radical critique of ruling-class history sought to redefine what aspects of *public* life were to be studied and was inclined to suspect the private as the baggage of privilege. While the aristocracy might have affairs, the working class did not.

From the 1960s, a new radical social history began to examine community and family life, but the real change in how 'the private' was regarded came in the 1970s, when the feminist movement in the United States, adopting the slogan of the radical student movement, rebelled by insisting that the personal was political. This was to be interpreted in several ways. It enlarged the area of private experience that could be incorporated into how knowledge was publicly constituted, and it challenged the magisterial removal of a personal stance from how the world was seen. In the past thirty years, a feminist-influenced history, especially in the US, where women's history conferences can number 4,000 and generate a vast market for books, has had an extraordinary impact. Bodies, housework, sex and shopping are as much part of this history as work, social policy and politics.

The personal as political happened to fit the aspirations of feminists at a particular period – so much so that it has become seen as something inherent in feminism. In fact, the maxim struck a chord only in certain feminisms, and the widespread assumption that it can be equated with feminism in all cultures and all periods is a misapprehension. In France, for example, the mainstream of the women's movement was wary of this merging of the personal and public, perhaps raising a deeper issue about cultural differences. In France, private life is assumed to influence public life but behind firmly closed doors.

The redefinition of the public to include aspects of private life, which received such an impetus from American feminism, has been part of a much longer cultural shift. Its roots can be found in the Victorian Anglo-Saxon moral concern to match public pronouncements with personal behaviour. Witness the storm that followed James Anthony Froude's biographical revelations in the early 1880s that Thomas Carlyle had neglected and verbally abused his wife Jane. How could a really great man be revealed as churlish and mean? What aspects of private life mattered? What were the general public entitled to know?

Froude's new approach to biography appeared at a time when the Church, which had marked out the paths of correct personal action, was seeing its authority being nibbled away. Judgement became something of a free-for-all. By the early twentieth century, the avant-garde were contesting ideas of good and bad in personal life. The tolerant ethics that writer E.M. Forster displays in novels such as *Howards End* and *A Passage to India* were based not on an external moral standard but on a sense of the inner authenticity of his characters' actions. His concern with personal relations represented a kind of working compromise in a period when an interest in psychology was probing motives and turning moral certainties on their head. The same fascination with the subjective was to bring many aspects of behaviour – including of course sex – out into the public arena.

So, challenging the boundaries between private and public was already an aspect of modern society before feminism. What is certainly true, however, is that the tendency to push more and more aspects of life into the public domain has accelerated. What would Froude have made of *Hello!* magazine? one wonders. Many of the questions his work raised are still current. When Diana, Princess of Wales, died, an anxiety about the extent to which the private lives of celebrities should be scrutinised in public swept through the British media. Whereas the increased visibility of personal life had been largely seen as part of a growing acceptance within the public sphere of diversity and tolerance, Diana's death caused the more sinister implications of revelation to become evident.

For not all aspects of the fusion of the personal and the public are necessarily benign. People who have lived through periods in which the state impinges on personal life know all about this. Russian dissidents who had seen parents denounced by their children wanted to keep the private apart from the public. French Revolutionary women in the 1790s, who could be denounced for a liking for musk perfume, probably had a similar wish as they headed towards the guillotine.

The private sphere, moreover, contains particular perils for women. Confined to a domestic role, middle-class Victorian women were idealised as angels of the hearth; modern feminist academics have metamorphosed this despised 'hearth' into the realm of private subjectivity. While 1970s feminist theory sought to bring the private into politics, feminist academics now are likely to focus on subjectivity and forget the politics. The result has been both creative innovation and an excruciating preoccupation with the person who is writing at the expense of the topic at hand. The negative consequences have been a double restriction. Firstly, a notion of 'feminist' methodology distinguishes and encloses the female researcher within a separate approach to knowledge rather than challenging the bias in how culture is defined as a whole, leaving the chaps to get on with the 'real' stuff of history. Secondly, concentration on private life is inclined to divorce women from a broader perspective of social and political processes.

Such an extreme preoccupation with the private now exists that a new *balance* is called for between the private and the public. Marx's neglect of the influence of the subjective, along with his neglect of domestic activity, are evident deficiencies; on the other hand, a critical use of Marxism remains a rich mine for thinking about questions which are left out by both the history that focuses on the lives of the great and by exclusive preoccupation with subjectivity and the private sphere. How, for example, can historians account for the complex interactions of a vast multitude of subjectivities upon social life? If we are to understand politics as influenced by movements from below, rather than simply steered by those at the top, this is an inescapable historical question.

Current fashions for the lives of the great on the one hand, or for private life and personal stance on the other, do not trouble me because they include the private as significant. I think it is indeed significant. My dissatisfaction stems from the former's denial of subjectivity to all but great ladies, and the tendency of the latter to dump political and social action, or even aspects of existence such as work, as outside the scope of inquiry.

Further reading

Shirley Harrison: *Sylvia Pankhurst: A Crusading Life, 1882–1960* (Aurum Press, 2003)

Yvonne Kapp: *Eleanor Marx, vols 1 and 2* (Lawrence & Wishart, 1972 and 1976)

Meredith Kwartin Rusoff: 'R.H. Tawney and the WEA', in Stephen K. Roberts (ed.), *A Ministry of Enthusiasm: Centenary Essays on the Workers' Educational Association* (Pluto Press, 2003)

D.J. Trela: 'Froude on the Carlyles: The Victorian Debate over Biography', in Kristine Ottesen Garrigan (ed.), *Victorian Scandals: Representations of Gender and Class* (Ohio State University Press, 1992)

Barbara Winslow: *Sylvia Pankhurst: Sexual Politics and Political Activism* (UCL Press, 1996).

Commentary by Mandy Garner
Features editor of the Times Higher Education Supplement

In today's celebrity age, it is no surprise that current trends in history reflect interest in the personal. Many historians would argue that this corrects an earlier imbalance towards the public and wider social sphere, but in recent years questions have been asked about whether we are in danger of indulging our interest in gossip to the detriment of wider analysis.

Since ancient times, thinkers have shown an interest in the lives of the 'great and good'. From works such as Virgil's *Aeneid*, which sought to explain the history of the foundation of Rome through stories about mythical figures, to religious scholars in the Middle Ages writing about the lives of saints, writers showed an interest in mixing the personal with wider historical developments. But in the post-Enlightenment period, as history began to emerge as a discipline in its own right, historians began to focus more on broader social themes and trends. Immanuel Kant (1724–1804) argued that social progress could only be seen if the history of man was viewed over a large time span, rather than in the lives of individuals. For Karl Marx, economics was the powerhouse of history, while this interest in broader patterns was taken up in the twentieth century by the *École des Annales*, which rejected the traditional focus of history on facts and events in favour of the broader sweep, bringing other humanities – principally the social sciences – to the fore to create 'a larger and a more human history'. The result was a greater focus on areas such as agriculture and the environment.

In the 1960s, however, *annalistes* turned away from economics and social science to embrace subjects like anthropology and sociology and what was called 'the history of mentalities'. This was a more extreme reaction to the traditional history of events, and saw the whole of history as a construct of human impressions. The focus was on everyday life, the history of traditions and customs and how they had evolved slowly over time.

One reason for this shift was the influence of Sigmund Freud (1856–1939), who had much to say, particularly in the later stages of his life, on what he saw to be the motivating forces of history. Although sympathetic to Marxism, he felt it could not wholly explain the evolution of civilisation, since it ignored psychological factors. In *Civilization & Die Weltanschauung* (1918), he argues: 'It cannot be assumed that economic motives are the only ones which determine the behaviour of men in society. The unquestionable fact that different individuals, races and nations behave differently under the same economic conditions in itself proves that economic factors cannot be the sole determinant. It is quite impossible to understand how psychological factors can be overlooked where the reactions of living human beings are involved; for not only were such factors already concerned in the establishment of these economic conditions but even in obeying these conditions, men can do no more than set their original instinctual impulses in motion – their self-preservative instinct, their love of aggression, their need for love and their impulse to attain pleasure and avoid pain.'

A key exponent of the new emphasis on the individual was Philippe Ariès, best known for the way he broadened out the themes historians could tackle – from family life, to sexuality, to death. Key texts include his 1960 study of attitudes towards the family and childhood, *Centuries of Childhood: A Social History of Family Life*, in which he uses diaries and cultural artefacts, such as paintings, to piece together a detailed picture of change over the centuries, and for his 1977 book on attitudes towards death and dying, *The Hour of our Death*. His *Western Attitudes Towards Death: From the Middle Ages to the Present* develops the hypothesis that changes in gravestone inscriptions and monuments reveal a 'psychoanalysis of history'. In his view, Western societies constructed a series of defences against nature, seeking to restrain sex and death through taboos or rituals that subjected the individual to the concerns of the collective.

Over his career, Ariès became more and more interested in the role of collective memory – the 'collective non-conscious' – in shaping traditions and customs. In this, he foreshadowed work by cultural historians in the 1980s on the role of memory in history, including Pierre Nora's eight-year project on the French national memory, *Rethinking France*, to which many French historians contributed, and which was remarkable for its attempt to break down the single narrative of history. The essays take as their point of departure a *'lieu de mémoire'* – a site, political tradition, ritual, or even national pastime or textbook. In the UK, historians such as

Simon Schama have also been keen to investigate the role of memory in history – Schama's 1995 book *Landscape and Memory*, for instance, explores the myths that have transformed Western culture.

By the 1980s and 1990s, when Ariès and fellow *annaliste* Georges Duby edited the huge *History of Private Life* series, which extends back to ancient Rome and has become a standard of cultural history courses, family history, including tracing family trees and television sagas on historical figures, had become big business both inside and outside academia. Big rows have enveloped historians such as Harvard's Steven Ozment who stated that parents in pre-modern times loved their children, and that husbands and wives sometimes cared for each other. His views broke with those of academics from the Sentiments School, who based their ideas on Ariès' book on childhood. According to Ariès, parents in the premodern period saw their children as little adults, and childhood as we know it today only emerged when families stopped sending young children outside the home to work. British historian Lawrence Stone's 1977 book, *The Family, Sex, and Marriage in England, 1500–1800*, developed Ariès' ideas into a sharply delineated scheme of family evolution. He spoke of the English family of the 1450–1630 period as being characterised by 'distance, manipulation, and deference'. Ozment's views come mainly from research into letters and other material from literate upper- and middle-class families, rather than statistical data. He argues that his research is deeper, if perhaps not quite as broad as that which cites statistical studies. 'I would much rather generalise from a handful of people in a particular place than rely on a shallow survey of what seems to lie on the surface,' he told the *Harvard Gazette*.

Interest in family and domestic matters perhaps reflects increasing individualism in Western society. Steven Mintz, director of the American Cultures Program at the University of Houston, and an authority on the history of families and children, writes on the university's digital history site: 'Today's history needs to reflect the preoccupations of our time. We live in an age preoccupied with issues of identity and intimacy. We need a history that places those concerns in historical perspective. What I am going to suggest to you is that the history of the family or manners or sports is as worthy of study as the 30 Years War.'

Allied to this interest in the personal and in memory has come a rise in the academic study of oral history. At Indiana University, the Oral History Project was set up in 1968, mainly to study the history of the university. This was soon expanded, and in 1981 it was renamed the Oral History Research Center, its scope being broadened to encompass the study of twentieth-century history through first-person testimony. In 2002, the centre expanded again to take on the growing interdisciplinary field of memory studies.

The move towards the personal has not necessarily brought a depoliticisation of history. Quite the contrary. Part of the movement away from broader-sweep views of history was driven by the civil rights and feminist movements. Moves to include groups that had not traditionally attracted the attention of historians brought a questioning of the values that underlay classical traditions of historical study. For historians, the feminist mantra of 'the personal is political' was to bring not just new actors into the historical arena, but also new topics for investigation, as well as new ways of looking at old subjects. Feminist historians such as Carolyn Steedman, for instance, look at the history of the shaping of masculine and feminine identities, mainly by class. In recent years, the tables have been turned on the public/private debate, with historians such as Earl Lewis and Bonnie Smith seeking to show how men's sense of identity comes from the family, while women's comes from work. In an essay published in *What is History Now?* (2002), Alice Kessler-Harris comments: 'When we watch public and private dissolve into each other, we are led to ask questions about the political purposes and subjective self-interest inherent in constructing oppositional spheres, like family and employment, or home and politics, in tension with each other. What nexus of power does such restricted vision sustain?'

Similiarly, historians of black history have sought to dissect traditional histories of the world in order to show how they have excluded those deemed of little interest. The result has been a questioning of history, of its role, of whether it can ever be anything more than a subjective activity, based on the interests of those writing it, of whether it is in fact anything more than a story.

For many, such questioning has had a positive impact, but some are now starting to debate the extent to which the personal and subjective has entered history, leading to an 'anything goes'

Big Questions in History

mentality. In a speech to the Institute of Historical Research in 2002, Eric Hobsbawm pointed to some of the dangers of associating history too closely with issues of identity and roots, saying that it could lead to 'in-group history – history fully accessible only to those who share the historical and life experience of its subject, or even the physical configuration of the humans to whom it appeals'. This, he said, 'undermines the universality of the universe of discourse that is the essence of history as a scholarly and intellectual discipline. It also undermines what both the ancients and the moderns had in common, namely the belief that historians' investigations, by means of generally accepted rules of logic and evidence, distinguish between fact and fiction, between what can be established and what cannot, what is the case and what we would like to be so.' This was increasingly dangerous in the modern world where 'more history than ever is today being revised or invented by people who do not want the real past, but only a past that suits their purpose'.

How do physical bodies affect cultural change

How do physical bodies affect cultural change?

Joanna Bourke
Professor of history at Birkbeck College, London

In archives, historians encounter the things that people in the past have left behind. When we spill the contents of a life on to the desk, split open the envelopes, turn the pages of the secret diary and read an individual's account of some event, word becomes flesh. History is fundamentally about the fleshiness, and therefore the precariousness, of humanity.

Yet, until recently, historians have been reluctant to allow the body into their learned annals. Separation of the social and biological sciences disciplines and an insistence on the need to privilege reason have ensured that visceral forces in human history are sidelined. Within the modern Western tradition of mind-body dualism, historians have tended to insist that the proper focus of their research should be culture, not nature. Since human physiology is often thought to be natural and static over time, attempts to engage with somatic aspects of lived experience are seen as reductionist. But jettisoning those seemingly passive endowments of bodily powers, movements and sensory facilities, has disembodied historical actors. Individuals and groups in the past become ethereal cultural and economic subjects in trousers and skirts, calmly calculating social risk in the slums of Salford or the bogs of Donegal. For these hardline social constructionists, 'discourse' rules. The body is presented as being wholly constructed by cultural regimes of power, keeping the individual in thrall to disciplining discourses and institutions.

Nevertheless, for all individuals, the body remains

the site of direct experience. Life, indeed all of history, is experienced through somatic responses. Irrespective of conscious desire, people are betrayed by physiology in terms of respiration, circulation, digestion and excretion. This is not to go to the other extreme and deny that bodies are constituted within temporal and social space. While illness is undoubtedly a physiological process, the meaning ascribed to any illness is not only integral to the disease but also to the experience of illness. Thus, tuberculosis is caused by the organism mycobacteria, but tuberculosis sufferers might feel romantic, sensitive and beautiful if they lived in the nineteenth century, or dirty, impoverished and stigmatised if living in the late twentieth century.

Therefore, historians should adopt an 'aesthesiological' approach to people in the past – that is, an approach that acknowledges the history of bodily and emotional reactions to the world. After all, frightened people possess a body – witness the trembling of limbs and hysterical gait of the survivors of disasters. Although there is a theatre to the physiology of fear – with executives acting out anxiety neuroses while their employees revel in the drama of hysteria – it is not always choreographed according to any predetermined schema of class, gender or ethnicity. Discourse shapes bodies but bodies also shape discourse: people are 'weak or pale with fright', 'hot with anger', 'flushed with love'. Meaning and metaphor derive from our bodily experience. The body, by shaping articulate experience, influences that experience.

It is patently the case that we are bodies, as well as having them. There is no clear division between the physical body and the communicative or 'lived' body, or, in other words, between biology and culture. The social flows in our blood. Even historians who believe in the timeless universality of human physiology cannot deny the profound ways in which culture goes the way of all flesh. Culture takes life and shape in the body. Throughout history, interventions into physiological processes have been transforming. In the modern period, for instance, organ transplants, life-support systems, intravenous nutrition, dialysis and resuscitation techniques have provoked radically new confrontations with death. Older terrors about being wrongly declared dead (resulting in 'premature burial', which many nineteenth-century Britons feared) have become less meaningful than more recent anxieties of being wrongly obliged to stay alive (denied the opportunity to 'die with dignity').

More to the point, however, human physiology is simply not a historical constant. Biology is remarkably flexible. Contrary to the view that biology is fixed while culture is flexible, the former provides diverse potentials which the latter then selects and directs. The body is not a static object but incorporates synthetic components, such as silicone skins, cardiac pacemakers and artificial joints. Furthermore, the body's moral value and the value of its parts have undergone dramatic shifts over time. Changes in weight, height, hormonal levels, healthiness and life expectancy have all influenced cultural life in extraordinary ways. In part, these physiological changes were themselves an effect of cultural change (for instance, dietary modifications lowered the age of menstruation), but, in turn, they affected culture (by lowering the age of marriage). In other words, the body does not merely reflect societal processes, it also affects social processes. Culture acquires sense and meaning through embodiment. Without attributes of bodiliness, such as sensory faculties, meaning is impossible. Physical sensations are not merely the ornament of experience: they are the most irreducible 'real' of an individual's history.

Of course, as with all aspects of lived experience, the body enters the historical archive only to the extent to which it transcends individual sensation and presents the self within society. Thus, histories of the body (as with all histories) are dependent upon what is inscribed in public documents, including hospital and asylum records, governmental inventories, social inquiries, as well as in private letters, diaries and art. Through the analysis of these texts, historians are able to pursue fluctuations in the nature of the body. In this way, cultural language and rites expose everyday manifestations of fleshiness.

Such an aesthesiological approach to the body in history does not represent a retreat from politics, but a commitment to the lived experiences of subjects in the past. Indeed, the embodying process is precisely a rejection of historical writing that regards individuals as 'floating signifiers', vague 'others', or the historical profession's equivalent of the ventriloquist's doll. The historical body is not an empty, plastic entity but an active, forceful manipulator of the world. It moulds society, by limiting social change as well as by forcing through innovations. Karl Marx understood as much: bodily needs stimulate revolution. It is no coincidence that the sluggish, plump bodies of individuals in wealthy Western societies remonstrate in favour of consumer rights, while the emaciated proletariat of the nineteenth century rioted in protest against wage levels and employment practices.

In this way, the body is crucial to understanding regimes of power. Bodies have always been at the heart of social power. Lived experience is not only about the individual body, for the body is fundamentally experienced in relation to other bodies and environments. It is the medium through which social agency is exercised. Lived experience is felt, and although experience cannot be reduced to physical sensations, nevertheless, it is not 'lived' without sensation. Social theory necessarily concerns itself with bodies because bodies are the chief medium of social reproduction and cultural expression. Within the archive, the historian bears witness to past individuals as living, active flesh.

Further reading

Joanna Bourke: *Fear: A Cultural History of the Twentieth Century* (Virago, 2004)

Paul Hirst and Penny Woolley: *Social Relations and Human Attributes* (Tavistock Publishers, 1982)

Thomas Laqueur: *Making Sex: Body and Gender from the Greeks to Freud* (Harvard University Press, 1990)

Bryan Turner: *The Body and Society: Explorations in Social Theory* (Blackwell, 1984)

Simon Williams: *Emotion and Social Theory: Corporeal Reflections on the (Ir)Rational* (Sage, 2001).

Commentary by Claire Sanders
Writer on the Times Higher Education Supplement

It is a sad irony that the historian most associated with the history of the body – in Britain at least – dramatically suffered the failure of his own body aged just fifty-five. Within months of retiring from his job as professor at the Wellcome Trust Centre in 2001, Roy Porter was found dead next to his bicycle on his way to his allotment after suffering a heart attack.

As one reviewer, Lisa Jardine, put it, his book, *Flesh in the Age of Reason*, published posthumously in 2003, presented 'a vivid picture of how modern accounts of the paradoxical relationship between bodily organs and informing sensibility developed, tracing lucidly the transformation of the pre-modern rational soul into a peculiarly modern subjectivity and sense of self'.

Porter's book fleshed out the Enlightenment, even placing the great thinkers of the time clearly in their own suffering bodies. So we find that Edward Gibbon (1737–1794), author of *Decline and Fall of the Roman Empire*, was known unkindly as Chubby-Chubb to his colleagues. And that the thinker who liked to describe his body as a 'machine' – 'subordinate and disciplined' – experienced his body cruelly reasserting its presence in the form of a hydrocele – an enlargement of the scrotum. 'Gibbon tells readers he is giving them the "naked truth", but his relationship to his body was evidently unresolved, and the naked flesh does not come across in his memoirs,' wrote Porter. 'For while he refers to his gout (a good disease), he does not mention the complaint which indirectly killed him – his hydrocele.'

Christian theology, with its soul-body dualism, had long kept the body at arm's length. Fear of the corrupting influence of the flesh underlay much Christian thinking, most notably that of the influential Augustine (354–430). As Porter illustrated, the great Enlightenment thinkers who sought to escape the constraints of religion, and in so doing questioned the whole notion of a soul, similarly struggled to subordinate the body – this time to the mind, the emerging rational self. The result was that before the mid twentieth century the body was rather incidental to history, with historians prioritising spiritual and mental aspects of culture.

Today, historians ignore the body at their peril. Writing in the *Companion to Medicine in the Twentieth Century* (2000), Mark Jenner and Bertrand Taithe observe: 'In the past 15 years "the history of the body" has become fashionable to the point of ubiquity.' But while Porter and the Cambridge sociologist Bryan Turner are often credited with introducing the body to history, it was not entirely ignored by earlier historians. Jenner and Taithe, arguing that 'claims to novelty are greatly exaggerated', point to the first generation of the *annales* school of French historians, writing between the wars, as being particularly concerned with bodies. 'You will find few finer examples of "body history" than Marc Bloch's discussion of medieval and early monarchs' claims to heal scrofula by touching the afflicted, or Lucien Febvre's evocations of the sensory world of the 16th century,' they suggest.

Other disciplines have also crossed over into history in this area. Particularly influential in the history of the body is French philosopher Michel Foucault (1926–1984), who challenged assumptions about mentally ill people, prisons, and the rise of medicine and hospitals, and whose *History of Sexuality* traces the development of subjectivity and explores new ways of relating to self. Another important influence is anthropologist Mary Douglas, who in her 1966 book *Purity and Danger*, looks at why certain things in different societies are considered 'clean' while others are regarded as polluted, and how religion and ritual reinforce the message. Jenner and Taithe also cite earlier anthropologists – in particular Bronislaw Malinowski (1884–1942), whose work included examinations of sexual taboos and science; Marcel Mauss (1872–1950), who looked at the relationship between anthropology and psychology; and Margaret Mead (1901–1978), whose work on gender differences, child rearing and sexuality retained a 'profound focus on the body'. And, over the past twenty-five years, the physical condition of the body has been important for economic and historical demographers too.

Explaining the reach of the *Companion*, editors Roger Cooter and John Pickstone, write: 'Although the body now features prominently in the titles of hundreds of social, historical, and anthropological studies of medicine and culture, we use it here to include not only the corporeal/material entity that has long been at the centre of the medical gaze, but also the lay and professional packages (and packers) of knowledge that have contributed to the making of the human body over the course of the century.'

Porter had his own way of contrasting the material entity with the 'packers'. In *Blood and Guts: A Short History of Medicine*, he observes, 'The body is pregnant with symbolic meanings, deep, intensely charged and often highly contradictory. For orthodox Christians, for instance, being originally made in God's image, it is a temple. Yet since the Fall and expulsion from the Garden of Eden, bodies have been "vile" and the flesh weak and corrupt. Medical beliefs are always underpinned by cultural attitudes and values about the flesh.' Equally, he observes, all societies from earliest times have had 'some tangible knowledge of the innards'. Histories of the body reflect this, covering a spectrum from works most concerned with the symbolism and cultural context of the body to those preoccupied with the material reality of the 'innards' – the latter most commonly falling in the realm of straightforward medical histories.

Take the history of sexuality, which tends to fall at the cultural end of the spectrum. In 1899, the sexologist Havelock Ellis remarked: 'In no other field of human activity is so vast an amount of strenuous didactic morality founded on so slender a basis of facts . . . often ostentatiously second-hand, usually unreliable.' In the *Companion*'s chapter on the sexual body, Lesley Hall says Foucault's *History of Sexuality* 'made the important (though not entirely original) point that sexuality is discursively produced; that is, it is something which is formed by what people say and think about the bodily phenomena involved rather than simply emerging from a set of physical processes'. And for some, even those physical processes have not been straightforward. In *Making Sex: Body and Gender from the Greeks to Freud* (1990), Thomas Laqueur argues that in the late eighteenth century there was a significant shift in perceptions of male and female. According to Laqueur, the 'one-sex model', where the female organs were seen as interior versions (or inside-out versions) of the male equivalents, was superseded by a 'two-sex model', where the two sexes were seen as completely different.

The end of the spectrum more concerned with unravelling the mystery of the 'innards' – the material entity – has often related a story of progress, of optimism. This is sometimes attributed to the dominance of scientists and medical practitioners over the history of their fields.

One of the earliest and most influential was the ancient Greek physician to the gladiators, Galen, who looked back to Hippocrates, credited with the idea of four bodily humours needing to be in balance. Galen's numerous works integrating philosophy and medicine dominated medical history to the Renaissance and beyond, just as his work on dissection influenced medical practice. Among those he influenced was the eleventh-century Persian physician Avicenna. His many works included a *Canon* of medicine and he was particularly interested in psychology. Another Galen follower was the fourteenth-century Italian physician Mondino de Luzzi, author of *Anatomia Mundini*, which became a standard text. But in 1543, Andreas Vesalius' beautifully illustrated *De Fabrica Corporis Humani* took the Greeks to task for relying on their knowledge of animal and not human bodies. This chiding was continued by William Harvey, a yeoman's son who graduated from Cambridge in 1597 and went on to discover our circulatory systems. Harvey wrote: 'I profess to learn and teach anatomy not from books but from dissections; not from the tenets of philosophers but from the fabric of nature.'

Early modern writing on the history of medicine was dominated by collections of the great texts and the lives of great doctors, always emphasising the advancement of knowledge, in keeping with Enlightenment values. The notion of progress continued well into the nineteenth and twentieth centuries. Recent medical history, however, has become more ambiguous about the issue. James Le Fanu's gloomy book *The Rise and Fall of Modern Medicine* (1999) claims that after great advances in the second half of the twentieth century medical progress has now ground to a halt. He argues that the twin hopes of epidemiology and the genome revolution have failed to deliver. For Porter, too, writing in *The Greatest Benefit to Mankind*: 'Medicine's finest hour is the dawn of its dilemmas. With mission accomplished its triumphs are dissolving in disorientation.'

As writers of medical history have challenged the assumption of medical advances, writers of histories of the body have challenged the assumption that bodies can be written about in the abstract, without acknowledging that they belong to people we love. In *The*

Lunar Men: The Friends who Made the Future (2003), Jenny Uglow describes the public dissections of human bodies by Erasmus Darwin, who, in common with many other medical men of the time, used the bodies of executed prisoners. 'Tyburn relatives would cling to the feet of the hanged men to prevent them being carried to the surgeon's hall,' writes Uglow. Already, the medical need to understand was in conflict with the desire of relatives to cherish the body of a loved one, but this is only now beginning to be recognised by historians. As Jenner and Taithe put it: "We have next to no historical discussions of the body of the loved one – parent, child or partner – (as opposed to the sexual body). This is all too often a historiography largely devoid of tenderness, of affection and indeed of respect.'

What is the impact of geography on events

What is the impact of geography on events?

Felipe Fernández-Armesto

Prince of Asturias Professor at Tufts University and a professorial fellow of Queen Mary, University of London

? By the standards of astrophysicists, say, or science-fiction writers, historians seem unadventurous – interested only in one puny species on one tiny planet. But earth is special, with a crammed, teeming biosphere. So far, we know of nowhere else in the cosmos where so much happens.

The human part of the story is of consuming interest to us. We usually call it history, but we might as well call it human geography or a branch of environmental studies, for, in isolation, humankind makes imperfect sense. To comprehend our history, we need to study it in the contexts from which it is truly inseparable: the climates that surround it, the soils and seas on which it happens, and the other life forms on which we depend or with which we compete.

This means restoring history and geography to each other. All disciplinary boundaries should be uncongenial to historians, who want to embrace the whole of the past, including the past of every art and science. But the 'Anglo-Saxon attitude' that confines geographers and historians to mutually uncommunicating departments is particularly uncongenial, if we like peopled landscapes and contextualised lives.

Homo sapiens is an exceptionally successful species, able to survive in a wide range of climates and landscapes – more so than just about any other creature, except for the microbes we carry around with us. But even we are still explorers of our planet, engaged in an unfinished effort to change it. Indeed, that effort has barely begun, though some human societies have devoted the past 10,000 years or so to it. We call ourselves 'lords of creation' or, more modestly, its 'stewards', but about 90 per cent of the biosphere is too far underwater or too profoundly subterranean for us to inhabit with our current technology: these are environments that humans have only recently begun to invade and that we still do not dominate.

We are ambitious, by comparison with other animals, in remodelling the earth to suit our own purposes: we carve up fields, turn prairies into wheatlands, deserts into gardens and paradise into desert; we fell forests where we find them, and plant them where none exists; we dam rivers, wall seas, extinguish some species and call others into being by selection and hybridisation. Sometimes we smother terrains with new environments that we build for ourselves. Yet none of these practices liberates us from nature.

One of the paradoxes of the human story is that the more we intervene to change the environment, the more vulnerable we become to ecological lurches and disasters and unpredictable effects. We lord it over other species, but we remain linked to them by the food chain. We transform our environment, but we can never escape from it.

So if we neglect geography, in the broadest sense of the word, we neglect the framework of everything else that happens to us. The notion that chaps and maps could be studied in separate departments now seems hopelessly old-fashioned. Geography has been transformed in my lifetime by the influence of environmental science. History is now catching up. Insights from ecology are revolutionising the way we look at our past, making historians aware, for instance, of how the cycles of global warming and cooling, the fluctuations of regional weather systems and the 'oscillation' of currents have influenced migrations, wars, famines, gluts and the fates of states and civilisations.

History has to be about climate because,

although climate determines nothing, it conditions everything. It has to be about winds and currents because, throughout the age of sail – that is, for almost the whole of recorded history – they channelled and funnelled long-range communications. In most history books, there is too much hot air and far too little wind. Environmental science should inform economic history because all the resources we exploit, exchange or exhaust are wrested from the earth and the atmosphere. History has to be about landscape because the recrafting of landscape has been the great common project of humankind since the domestication of fire.

Every history student should now appreciate that alongside the great political, social, economic and intellectual revolutions that we have traditionally used to characterise modernity, we have to place the ecological revolution that we commonly call 'the Columbian exchange'. For, over the past five hundred years, the swapping of biota across oceans and between continents has reversed a pattern of evolution prevalent since the sundering of the original super-continent, Pangaea. A divergent pattern, which made the life forms of the continents ever more different from one another, has been replaced by a convergence of species all over the world.

There is growing recognition of the importance of food for the understanding of everything else in history – and rightly so, because nothing matters more than food to most people in most cultures for most of the time. And the history of food is, above all, a subject of historical ecology. People are at their most dependent and their most destructive and therefore are most intimately involved with the rest of nature when they eat it. The stories of herding and farming – the dominant stories in the histories of peoples since the ice age – are of human interventions in the processes of evolution and of growing interdependence between humans and other species. Agricultural revolutions underpinned the rise of the 'great civilisations' of antiquity, the prosperity of high-medieval Eurasia, the world hegemony of the modern West.

One of the consequences of our developing food technologies has been the history of new eco-niches in which diseases breed, with powerful consequences for human societies. Micro-organisms that bear disease constantly limit and liberate human potential. Increasingly, we are coming to realise that our medical history is not a one-sided story of the failures and triumphs of human agency: the mutations of microbial evolution play an ineluctable part in it, unleashing and ending 'ages of plague'. History has to be about microbes as well as men, because the former infest the latter, shaping our lives, determining our deaths.

Finally, modern trends in science and philosophy have combined to remind us that humans are animals – part of the great animal continuum; like other animals, we are best studied in our habitats. This suggests to me that we should prepare for another revolution in historiography – one that will, I suspect, be informed by insights from the study of non-human societies, and especially from primatology. To understand ourselves thoroughly, and to know what, if anything, makes us unique, we have to compare ourselves with other animals.

If humans are peculiarly ambitious creatures, who are always intervening in the life of the planet, we are also odd compared with other animals in the way we generate change among ourselves. We are a volatile, unstable species. Other animals live social lives and construct societies. But those societies are remarkably stable compared with ours. As far as we know, ants and elephants have the same ways of life and the same kinds of relationships as they have had since their species first emerged.

Some other creatures have cultures that change. One of the fascinating discoveries of late twentieth-century primatology is that apes and monkeys develop cultural differences from one another, even between groups living in similar and sometimes adjacent environments. In one forest region of Gabon, chimpanzees have developed termite-catching technology – they 'fish' with stripped branches that they plunge into termite nests – but do not use tools to break open nuts; in a neighbouring region, they ignore the termites, but have developed expertise in nut-cracking with rocks that they use as hammers and anvils. In Sumatra, orang-utans play a game – jumping from falling trees – that is unknown to their cousins in Borneo. In some baboon groups in Ethiopia's highlands, males control harems; in others in nearby savannah, they practise 'serial monogamy'. Primatology allows us to see what makes human history distinctive and, therefore, objectively interesting.

In a sense, all history is historical ecology. This does not mean it has to be materialist, because many of our interventions in the environment start in our minds, in our habit of self-distancing from the rest of nature. Like the geometry of civilisations, they are imagined or devised before they happen outwardly. Cities are underlain by ideals of order, agriculture by visions of abundance, laws by hopes of utopia, writing by a symbolic imagination, technology by an urge to improve on nature, science by Faustian temptations to control it. Mind and body are symbiotic. We can understand the scope of spirit and intellect best when we locate them in the grid and grit of the material world, where they belong but where they are not confined.

Further reading

A.W. Crosby: *The Columbian Exchange: Biological and Cultural Consequences of 1492* (Greenwood Press, 1972); *Ecological Imperialism: The Biological Expansion of Europe 900–1900* (Cambridge University Press, 1986)

Jared Diamond: *Guns, Germs and Steel* (W.W. Norton, 1997)

Felipe Fernández-Armesto: *Civilizations* (Macmillan, 2000)

I.G. Simmons: *Environmental History: A Concise Introduction* (Blackwell, 1993)

Bert de Vries and Johan Goudsblom (eds): *Mappae Mundi: Humans and their Habitats in a Long-term Ecological Perspective* (Amsterdam University Press, 2002).

History is all about time and geography is all about space. That is the traditional demarcation line between the two subjects. But there has often been a crossover, and recently, aided by the fragmentation of most disciplines post postmodernism, the overlap has become increasingly marked, with geographers working within university history departments and vice versa. To some extent, this marks a return to a more classical age in which subjects were less neatly defined and thinkers roamed freely across their borders.

In early modern times, the German philosopher Johann Gottfried von Herder's 1781 book *Ideas for a Philosophical History of Mankind* brought together such apparently disparate subjects as geomorphology, astronomy, climate, geography and history, and stressed that all phenomena were interlinked, placing humankind at the centre of this network. His influence on subsequent thinkers, such as Georg Wilhelm Friedrich Hegel and Friedrich Nietzsche, and on developing ideas of nationalism in the nineteenth century, was enormous. His work also formed the basis for fields such as anthropology, which proved to have a significant influence on the development of cultural history in the twentieth century.

Another seminal figure was Robert Malthus (1766–1834), whose work linked a study of the history of traditional societies with issues such as population growth, agriculture and farming. Although many of his conclusions were later proven to be naive and ill-founded, he was one of the first historians to focus specifically on economic aspects of history – indeed his appointment in 1805 as professor of modern history and political economy at the East India Company's College in Haileybury made him England's first academic economist. Even Marx, who deplored the conservative conclusions of Malthus' influential 1798 *Essay on the Principle of Population* – that enriching the working classes would mean that population would outstrip food supply (his initial findings were later revised in line with empirical evidence to posit the idea that higher incomes might reduce fertility) – admitted that this was the first serious economic study of the welfare of the lower classes. Malthus' work, however outdated as Britain stood on the cusp of industrialisation, proved an inspiration for the social and economic historians who followed him.

In the early part of the twentieth century, the *École des Annales* in France rejected factual history in favour of a broader focus on the humanities, particularly geography and economics. One of its major figures, Fernand Braudel (1902–1985), sought to change the way historians focused on the world, shifting attention from rapid chains of events to deeper, slower trends over time that reflected the structures and circumstances that moulded society. Braudel, much influenced by *annales* founder Lucien Febvre (1878–1956), whose book *A Geographical Introduction to History* he read in 1924, attempted to add geographical considerations to the historian's traditional focus on time. In his *Mediterranean and the Mediterranean World in the Age of Philip II* (1949), he concentrated on how the environment of that region shaped its people, and how this influenced trading patterns and the development of capitalism. In this, he counterpointed long-term 'geographic time' against the more short-termist 'individual time'.

The *annaliste* influence is clear in E.H. Carr's 1961 book *What is History?*. He spoke of how 'history is the long struggle of man, by the exercise of his reason, to understand his environment and to act upon it'. In the modern period, he said, this also meant understanding oneself and being 'self-conscious and therefore conscious of history' and how it was shaped by a number of social factors. In the closing chapter, he spoke of how all the revolutions of the modern period were rooted in similar circumstances and were linked. 'The social revolution and the technological revolution and the scientific revolution are part and parcel of the same process,' he wrote, pointing out how industrialisation processes in Asia and Africa combined with growing educational and political consciousness could transform these continents, with what he called 'the expansion of reason' bringing a huge number of new actors into history.

According to Richard Evans, professor of modern history at Cambridge and author of the first article in this book, this emphasis on social science had, by the 1970s and 1980s, become too jargon-filled, too concerned with quantification and large trends, with the result that history's ability to communicate with a wider audience was damaged. 'Individual people all but disappeared from the historian's vision,' he says. Historians began to turn to other areas to reinvigorate their subject – and most specifically to culture. People were back, but instead of a return to leadership and 'great men' the focus was on ordinary people from all societies. This is where anthropology came into its own, and its influence on the development of cultural history – and geography – has been crucial in drawing the two subjects closer together. Similarly, the post-colonialist movement has reignited interest in other cultures and in the various ways that colonialism – the basis of modern geography, according to Anne Godlewska and Neil Smith's 1994 book *Geography and Empire* – has influenced the development of particular countries.

At the same time, historians have been grappling with the after-effects of postmodernism, which has led to increasing fragmentation of their subjects, and indeed to a questioning of the very nature of historical study. Geography similarly splintered into many parts in the last few decades of the twentieth century, feeding off some of the same intellectual environmental factors that had earlier shaped history – that is, the rise of postmodernism and 'hybrid' subjects such as sociology, cultural studies and anthropology, as well as the growing interest in the environment. Ron Johnston, professor of geography at Bristol University, says we now have an 'explosion' of specialisms within geography, from geopolitics and ancient geography to cultural and human geography. Distinctions between such specialisms grow ever more difficult to make.

In the 1990s, Simon Schama blurred the boundaries even more, bringing myth, art and landscape into the historical cauldron. His themes included the role of nature in the development of civilisations and the history of cultures. His 1995 book *Landscape and Memory* looks at the impact of culture on landscape and geography, and vice versa.

The publishing world has recently developed an interest in histories of cities or places, explicitly bringing concerns of time and place together, and in maritime history. Among the plethora of recent books on this subject is Exeter historian N.A.M. Rodger's *The Command of the Ocean: A Naval History of Britain 1649–1815*, which puts the structure and development of the navy at the heart of British history, showing how mutually dependent Britain and its navy became over this period. The book of the Institute of Historical Research's big Anglo-American conference in 2001, *Seafaring and*

Civilisation, by Philip de Souza, aims to explain why European empires dominated other seafaring nations. But it also tries to steer maritime history away from the study of naval battles and into wider development issues, covering everything from marine archaeology and the impact of sea transport on food and health to the spiritual and commercial ambitions on which European empires were built.

The subject to have a profound influence on both history and geography most recently is science, in keeping with our age of huge scientific change. It has influenced the type of subjects studied – from the environment to animal behaviourism – as Fernández-Armesto describes in the accompanying article, and spawned a spate of books looking at the history of particular inventions. Alan Macfarlane and Gerry Martin's 2002 book *The Glass Bathyscaphe*, for example, traces the impact glass has had on Western development, from medicine to agriculture. They state that 'glass did not force the amazing deepening of knowledge [in the Western world], but rather made it possible by providing new instruments: microscopes, telescopes, barometers, thermometers, vacuum flasks and many others. At a deeper level, it literally opened people's eyes and minds to new possibilities and turned Western civilisation from the aural to the visual mode of interpreting experience . . . The collapse of glass manufacture in Islamic civilisations and its decline in India, Japan and China made it impossible for them to have had the type of knowledge revolution that occurred in Western Europe'.

As forensics play an increasing role in history and some branches of geography become closely allied to statistics and mathematics, the techniques used by historians and geographers are also increasingly reflecting this scientific turn. And just as history and geography are being influenced by science, so subjects that were seen as scientific are taking on board history and geography. The geologist Richard Fortey, for example, has recently spoken out against those who would seek to impose a reductionist scientific approach on his subject. His approach is much more all-encompassing, relating geology to human culture and history. As Fortey says: 'I revel in the complexity of things.' Following the fragmentation and specialisation of the immediate postmodernist period, the time/place circle appears once again to be joined.

Can history have an end

Can history have an end?

Benjamin Barber
Distinguished university professor at the University of Maryland

The end of history recurs with some regularity. Every time a scholarly shill for the latest would-be empire decides his chosen people have a lock on tomorrow's hegemony stakes, he converts his wishful thinking into timeless stasis. If the 'victory' of capitalism over communism (*circa* 1990) meant the end of the cold war and hence the effective end of bipolar conflict, then America was surely about to become *numero uno* in a world of perpetual peace – the end of history as *pax Americana*.

This was more or less what Francis Fukuyama proposed in the 1990s (if with less enthusiasm than some of his critics realised) in the most recent proclamation of history's end. Georg Wilhelm Friedrich Hegel (1770–1831), Fukuyama's inspiration via the right-Hegelian Alexandre Kojève, had the same fantasy about his beloved Prussia, although it did not reciprocate his love until towards the end of his life, when he was finally given a coveted academic chair at Berlin. Like Fukuyama, Hegel was seduced by power – by Prussia's emerging status as a European worthy, if not quite a world colossus. But if Prussia could contend for Europe's leadership, and Europe was already the ruler of the world (*circa* 1830), then history might be regarded as approaching its appointed end, and the Owl of Minerva (bearing Hegel aloft) could finally take flight to survey the dusk marking the end of history's long day.

In contemplating time's end, Hegel had shrewdly observed that eras of peace were so many empty pages in history's annals. From this perspective, history might be said to terminate every time peace settles on humankind's raging passions – usually just for a fleeting moment, but occasionally for a bit longer. Yet conflict is our nature, and only observers of limited vision or historians of great expectations are likely to mistake a momentary pause in history's endless story of war for something more permanent.

Hegel at least indulged in speculating about an end to history as Europe entered a period of relative calm. Only a few small European wars, like the one in the Crimea and those permanent but one-sided colonial campaigns overseas, marred the long 'Congress of Nations' peace of the nineteenth century. And, yes to be sure, there were revolutions galore in 1830, 1848 and 1871 preparing for the BIG ONE in 1917 – but all in all a century far more tranquil than the one that had come before, and certainly no match for the one yet to come. If history was not exactly over, it seemed to be taking something of a snooze.

Fukuyama, on the other hand, mistook a mere moment of transient victory in the war between McWorld and jihad as the triumph of the one over the other. Even as writers like Robert Kaplan were detecting a rupturing of the nation state along ethnic and racial fissures, even as al-Qaeda was planning its first assault on the World Trade Center, even as the Balkans were unravelling and Hutus and Tutsis were setting about slaughtering one another, even as Samuel Huntington was predicting a wrenching clash of civilisations, Fukuyama was concluding that the collapse of the Soviets and the fall of the Wall marked not a momentary victory for American unipolarity – what the French came to call *hyperpuissance* – but the end of history. What he seemed to be saying, however, was not so much that history was over but 'we won'. Consequently, when 9/11 made it clear we had not won after all, the latest episode in the end of history came to an end.

More recently, with history again enthralled in

fits of hyperactivity, commentators have moved away from integration and stasis (the McWorld thesis) to give jihad and its cousins terrorism, civil war and anarchy their due. John Ralston Saul was found in *Harper's Magazine* proclaiming the 'end of globalization', while the prophets of American empire under siege and engaged in endless war rather than perpetual peace are being aptly represented in Clyde Prestowitz's *Rogue Nation* (2003), Chalmers Johnson's *The Sorrows of Empire* (2004), Zbigniew Brzezinksi's *The Choice* (2004) and my own *Fear's Empire* (2003).

Even in eras of peace, however, the notion that history can end is risible. It is not simply that apparent stillness usually covers a dialectical massing of forces along history's fragile tectonic plates, which are likely to give at some later point in a social earthquake; it is not just that, in the absence of war, social history of the kind laboriously chronicled by the *annales* school, where small changes in community behaviour – measured by minute entries in village registries – presage larger historical forces, keeps moving right along despite apparent stasis thank you very much. It is rather that the very idea of an end of history is rooted in an absurd and wholly implausible view of human nature.

History, after all, is but a reflection of human nature, and human nature is nothing if not contentious and quarrelsome (John Locke), a perpetual quest for power that ends only in death (Thomas Hobbes), men themselves being little more than 'voluble dissemblers anxious to avoid danger and covetous of gain' (Niccolò Machiavelli) who are likely to live in a condition where 'every man is enemy to every man . . .' where 'there is continual fear and danger of violent death; and the life of men, solitary, poor, nasty, brutish and short' (Hobbes again). We may thirst after Immanuel Kant's perpetual peace and Plato's eternal justice but, as Thrasymachus observes to Socrates, justice is usually but the right of the stronger. Even peace is the product of implied violence – that balance of terror about which Winston Churchill famously remarked: 'It may well be that we shall, by a process of sublime irony, have reached a stage where safety shall be the sturdy child of terror and survival the twin brother of annihilation.'

To make any real sense of the claim that history can end, we have then to raise the stakes. For it may be that seemingly silly aspirations to an end to history motivated by mere politics are informed by, and redolent of, a higher, more philosophical (even spiritual) quest for an end to multiplicity, tumult and the apartness that is life. From the start, thoughtful metaphysicians have imagined a yin and a yang – moments of stillness confronting moments of energy and movement – that constrain and impel the human story. The two Western philosophers who inaugurated this debate were Heraclitus (sixth century BC) for whom life was about difference, conflict and change; and Parmenides (fifth century BC), the champion of sameness, unity and stasis. For Parmenides, the world was one and oneness a form of motionlessness and hence timelessness (time *is* motion) in which neither difference nor change were real. Plato embraced Parmenides' aspirations but had finally to acknowledge that change (for him, dissolution) was ineluctable, the true way of the unhappy world.

Christianity bore witness to the same battle: man and woman given the gift of Eden, comfortable in God's timeless embrace, using (misusing) liberty to choose otherness – pushed by God to the hard world East of Eden where women would give birth in pain and suffering and men would labour by the sweat of their brows to earn the upkeep their burdensome mortality now laid on them. Welcome history, human time's big-bang beginning.

In the Christian story, however, painful as history may be, it is but an interval between timeless epochs of eternal rest. Representing apartness from God, it is a detour, a forced journey between the oneness from which humankind came and the redemption by which it was promised it might retrieve the eternal rest of reunion with the godhead. History and the Fall were one and the same, while salvation was the terminal way out. In this Christian perspective, the end of history is a feature of teleology: the idea that life's purposiveness is aimed at an end (*telos*) whose realisation both fulfils purpose and brings time to an end.

Hegel effectively rationalised the Christian teleology. In his metaphysic, profane history is driven by reason's sacred spirit towards a terminus that will be marked by timeless sublimity – although the realisation of spirit may be perpetually deferred by the intractable dialectics of real human life. Matthew Arnold (1822–1888) captures the paradox. Even as he gazed upon that relative century of peace that followed the Congress of Vienna, he had few doubts that as the gentle eternity that is love confronted the brute facts that are history, it would not be love that conquered. Be true to one another, he urges, 'for the world, which seems / To lie before us like a land of dreams, / So various, so beautiful, so new, / Hath really neither joy, nor love, nor light, / Nor certitude, nor peace, / nor help for pain; / And we are here as on a darkling plain / Swept with confused alms of struggle and flight, / Where ignorant armies clash by night.'

On the darkling plain of recent times, all the great utopians of the spirit have succumbed to a realism of the body. While they lend us hope that there may be ways to escape the darkling shadows, via therapy (Sigmund Freud), rationality (Max Weber) or revolution (Karl Marx), they recognise that conflict and life are the same. Id trumps superego, irrationality dominates reason, and power corrupts revolution. And so it seems, as long as we live and breathe, there will be conflict enough – war, cant, hatred, death and cruelty enough – to drive history forward.

The mundane *hegemon*'s dream of an end to history might then be generously understood as a secular version of the old dream of a return to Eden, a soft landing in God's bosom. It is the hope that telos might triumph over the teleological battles that are meant to produce it. As a religious and poetic reverie, it has much to recommend it.

As politics, however, it is more than dangerous. It mistakes momentary hegemonies like the current *pax Americana* for permanent peace, though such hegemonies are generally fated to provoke war just a stop or two down the line. In confounding God's grace with the construction of frail human empires, it invites disaster. In the end (which never comes), the boast that history is over, whether heard from the lips of Hegel, Marx or Fukuyama, seems all too familiar. Like George W. Bush's boast in 2003 that the war in Iraq was over, it is more often than not a prelude to hell rather than a gateway to heaven.

Further reading

Benjamin Barber: *Jihad Vs McWorld* (Ballantine, 1995)

Francis Fukuyama: *The End of History and the Last Man* (Avon, 1993)

Georg Wilhelm Friedrich Hegel: *Elements of the Philosophy of Right* (1820; Cambridge University Press, 1991)

Robert Kaplan: *The Ends of the Earth: A Journey at the Dawn of the 21st Century* (Random House, 1996)

Arnold Toynbee: (abridgement by D.C. Somervell) *A Study of History* (Oxford University Press, 1987).

Commentary by Harriet Swain
Deputy features editor of the Times Higher Education
Supplement

The end of history is not something many historians have been keen to contemplate. More often it has been the preserve of philosophers and political scientists, many with a particular point to prove. Indeed, the concept comes laden with all sorts of political and ideological baggage. Where a possible end *has* been identified, it has usually been as the destination of some kind of ideological journey rather than as a historical black hole.

For ancient historians the idea of an end to history was inconceivable. For them, the way human beings organised their affairs was cyclical. Polybius (*c.*200–118 BC) was one of the first to give a detailed explanation of this kind of historical cycle. He stated that there were six kinds of government, which occurred in succession – monarchy, tyranny, aristocracy, oligarchy, democracy and mob rule. The cycle began when natural disasters had wiped out the human race and when the survivors looked for a strong leader, and the only way out was a mixed constitution, incorporating monarchy, aristocracy and democracy. His ideas were revived in Renaissance Italy, with Niccolò Machiavelli agreeing that the 'perfect republic' was Rome, which he argued successfully achieved this mixed constitution.

Cyclical views of history have recurred in different guises and across different civilisations for centuries, from Ibn Khaldun's *Muqaddimah*, in the fourteenth-century Islamic world, to Giambattista Vico's notion of an 'eternal history' in eighteenth-century Italy, to nineteenth-century German philosopher Friedrich Nietzsche's idea of 'eternal recurrence', to Oswald Spengler's *Decline of the West* in post-First World War Germany, which drew analogies between the life cycles of different civilisations and the birth, life and death of living organisms.

Early linear views of history were usually linked to religion: Jewish, Muslim and Christian historians tended to see history as some kind of working out of a divine purpose, either manifested in a straight line from Creation to the Last Judgement or taking in various cycles of development and decline. For them, God would eventually supply history with an end. But in late seventeenth-century

Europe, in the atmosphere of secularism and scientific discovery that surrounded the Enlightenment, linear histories came to be associated with the notion of progress.

This kind of progress, which replaced God as the controller of human destiny with the exercise of human reason, took place predominantly among the *philosophes* of eighteenth-century France. It was perhaps best summed up in the work of the Marquis de Condorcet (1743–1794), whose *Sketch for a Historical Picture of the Progress of the Human Mind* was posthumously published in 1795. He described history as following a path of progress driven by the development of reason, in which man improved his knowledge of the natural world and how to manipulate it, increased tolerance and overcame superstition, and achieved greater equality among nations, and among men and women. These were ideas explored in different ways by Montesquieu, Voltaire and later by Auguste Comte (1798–1857), who argued that human thought passed through three stages – theological (dominated by superstition), metaphysical (where abstract thought begins) and positive (scientific) – in its journey from animal to human attributes.

In Britain, the idea of progress was most closely associated at this time with the 'Whig interpretation of history'. This was critically described by Herbert Butterfield in the book of that title in 1931 as 'the tendency in many historians to write on the side of Protestants and Whigs, to praise revolutions provided they have been successful, to emphasize certain principles of progress in the past and to produce a story which is the ratification if not the glorification of the present'. One of its main proponents was Thomas Babington Macaulay (1800–1859), who wrote in his *History of England*: 'The history of our country during the last 160 years is eminently the history of physical, of moral and of intellectual improvement.'

In Germany, Georg Wilhelm Friedrich Hegel (1770–1831) was displaying similar national pride, although he seemed to imply that, in his country, some sort of final historical goal had almost been reached. For him, history was the 'march of reason on the world' and its end the manifestation of Absolute Mind or Spirit. This Spirit had developed in stages from the Orientals, to the Greeks and Romans and finally the Germans: 'The history of the world is the discipline of the uncontrolled natural will, bringing it into obedience to a universal principle and conferring subjective freedom.

The East knew, and to the present day knows, only that *One* is free; the Greek and Roman world, that *some* are free; the German world knows that *all* are free.' Hegel believed that the state was key in this – 'the State is the idea of Spirit in the external manifestation of human Will and its freedom'. He argued that the impetus of historical development was dialectic: thesis and antithesis working together to produce a synthesis in a forward march to a greater truth.

Karl Marx (1818–1883) also adopted the dialectic method and the belief that it led to progress, but for him the driving force was not Spirit but economics, and its vehicle not the state but class. His 'materialist' concept of history divided human history into separate ancient, feudal and capitalist periods and foresaw a fourth – socialism, passing into the ideal, communism.

It was the interpretation of Hegel by a philosopher heavily influenced by Marx that inspired one of the most recent theories of historical progress – that of Francis Fukuyama. Fukuyama, a former policy adviser to American presidents Ronald Reagan and George Bush Sr, relied on Alexandre Kojève's take on Hegel when he declared the end of history. 'What we are witnessing is not just the end of the cold war, but the end of history as such: that is, the end point of mankind's ideological evolution and the universalisation of Western liberal democracy as the final form of human government.'

His thesis, first expressed in an article in 1989, has sparked controversy ever since. In 1991, York University professor Alex Callinicos argued that the upheavals at the end of the 1980s paved the way for more, rather than less, economic and political instability, which made the kind of communist society envisaged by Marx more necessary. Harvard political scientist Samuel Huntington's *The Clash of Civilizations* (1993) argues that the West is only one of several rival civilisations locked in a permanent struggle empowered by technology, while in *Jihad Vs McWorld* (1995) Benjamin Barber says that the kind of liberal democracy lauded by Fukuyama is being undermined by both capitalism and tribal and religious fundamentalism. Journalist Robert Kaplan's *The Coming Anarchy* (2001) refutes the idea that the cold war has brought global peace and prosperity and paints a disturbing picture of the future. Immanuel Wallerstein's *The Decline of American Power* (2003) suggests that America's days as a global power are numbered. And sociologist

Michael Mann has argued in *Incoherent Empire* (2003) that the 'new American imperialism' is in fact militarism that will increase world disorder.

Fukuyama came under particular fire following the World Trade Center attack in 2001. Ha, said the critics, where is your end of history idea now? Where it always was, Fukuyama replied coolly. In an article in the *Wall Street Journal* published shortly after the attack he repeated: 'We remain at the end of history because there is only one system that will continue to dominate world politics, that of the liberal-democratic West.'

Such a universal, politics-based view of history is a stark contrast to recent ways of thinking that have led to a very different concept of history's end. Postmodern approaches, which argue that historians are dependent on texts that are at the mercy of individual interpretations by both writer and reader, and that blur the distinction between history and fiction, have suggested to some that the idea of history is meaningless and its study no longer feasible. This does touch on the notion of 'end' as black hole rather than destination, although for some it has also been the beginning of new and stimulating ways of viewing the past. What it also shows clearly is that deliberations about the end of history come back, in cyclical fashion, to another key question: what is history?

Index

                               Big Questions in History